3

PRACTICAL
TAXIDERMY

COMMON PEAFOWL (Indo-China): Habitat group,
early morning. Mounted by the author from skins collected for group. (Field Museum of Natural History
photo)

PRACTICAL TAXIDERMY

Second Edition

JOHN W. MOYER
Former Staff Taxidermist
Field Museum of
Natural History

KRIEGER PUBLISHING COMPANY
MALABAR, FLORIDA

Original Edition 1953
Second Edition 1979
Reprint Edition 1992

Printed and Published by
KRIEGER PUBLISHING COMPANY
KRIEGER DRIVE
MALABAR, FLORIDA 32950

FROM A DECLARATION OF PRINCIPLES JOINTLY ADOPTED BY A COMMITTEE
OF THE AMERICAN BAR ASSOCIATION AND A COMMITTEE OF PUBLISHERS:

This publication is designed to provide accurate and authoritative information in regard to the
subject matter covered. It is sold with the understanding that the publisher is not engaged in
rendering legal, accounting, or other professional service. If legal advice or other expert
assistance is required, the services of a competent professional person should be sought.

Library of Congress Cataloging-In-Publication Data
Moyer, John W. (John William)
   Practical taxidermy / John W. Moyer. -- Reprint ed.
      p.   cm.
   Originally published: 2nd ed. New York : Wiley, 1979.
   Includes index.
   ISBN 0-89464-743-1
   1. Taxidermy. I. Title.
   [QL63.M67 1992]
   579'.4--dc20
                                                            92-4770
                                                            CIP

10   9   8   7   6   5   4   3

To all taxidermists, past and present

they who have worked diligently over the years
and with little remuneration
in creating wild-life as in nature

this book is humbly dedicated.

PREFACE

My first book, *Practical Taxidermy,* was published in 1953. In that book the subject of taxidermy was given by text, photographs, and drawings of methods in the art of taxidermy in use at that time. As with all subjects, techniques change, and today there are improved methods in "practical taxidermy" that have been developed since my first book came upon the market. This Second Edition will give some of these newer methods.

Not only has taxidermy advanced in its methods over the past years, but today there are more taxidermists practicing the art, either as a hobby, or both part-time and full-time as an income-producing profession. Only a few of these taxidermists, either commercial or museum, use the old "stuffing" methods, although, strange as it may appear to some, I have seen many fine mounts, especially in bird taxidermy, from the older methods.

In this, my newest offering, I have tried to search out and to give the more modern methods whereby birds, mammals, game heads, rugs, fish, and reptiles are mounted, either by sculptured forms, or by casts made from actual specimens. Taxidermy is not a secret art, and there is today a feeling of comradeship among most taxidermists that did not exist in years past. The only secret in taxidermy is in one's ability to study wildlife until one is versed in how birds and animals appear in nature. I can only give, to the best of my ability, known methods; you will have to supply the technique, knowledge, and craftsmanship in mounting the specimen of the wild with the correct anatomy, pose, and coloration.

Some taxidermists over past years have worked out other methods and techniques for the mounting of birds, mammals, fish, and other forms of wildlife. Some of these techniques are specialized and are used only for certain specimens, others result from the individual's way of working. (Some of these techniques have been issued in pamphlet form by the American Association of Museums; address requests to: American Association of Museums, 2233 Wisconsin Avenue, N.W., Washington, D.C. 20007.)

Very few books are written without the help and cooperation of others. In writing this book I am indebted to many who were my co-workers in years past and who helped me to learn the techniques of taxidermy—most of whom have passed on after leaving a life time of superb examples of the art of taxidermy. As I have been away from taxidermy for a number of years, I turned to the following for assistance in writing: to Jeff Cooper and Ken Motyka, who cooperated in allowing me to photograph the mounting of specimens in their studios; and to Jonas Brothers, Inc. (Denver), the Field Museum of Natural History (Chicago), and the Milwaukee Public Museum, for photographs. To all I am grateful. Without them there would have been no book.

JOHN W. MOYER

Michiana Shores, Indiana
November 1978

CONTENTS

PRACTICAL
TAXIDERMY

1 | INTRODUCTION: TAXIDERMY, YESTERDAY AND TODAY

The "art of taxidermy" is an art whose life has been short and, until a few years ago, uneventful when compared to the other so-called arts of music, painting, and sculpture. If taxidermy existed in ancient times there are no examples or writings to prove it. Taxidermy as practiced today differs in many ways from the taxidermy of years ago. Then, even though considered as some form of "art," it was in reality a "stuffing" process; today the taxidermist produces lifelike mounts of wildlife by modern methods of modeling the anatomy of birds and mammal specimens as they might appear in their natural habitat.

Taxidermy is the art of preserving the skin together with the feathers, fur, and scales of birds, animals, fish, and reptiles. The word is derived from two Greek words, *taxis* order, arrangement, preparation, and *derma* skin—a literal translation being the "skin art." The ancient Egyptians practiced a sort of taxidermy when they embalmed the bodies of dogs, cats, birds, and small animals, these being the pets of their rulers, and buried them in the tombs of the Pharaohs. This embalming was done by the injection of spices and oils and not by methods in use today. Many mummies, or preserved forms of such birds and animals, have been unearthed from the tombs and pits of Egypt and are on exhibit in museums. This embalming is simply a means of preservation and cannot, or should not, come under the art of taxidermy.

The Greeks and Romans also practiced a form of taxidermy in the tanning of skins used for clothing. Peoples inhabiting ancient Britain and other northern lands had no other means of covering their bodies and skins of lions, tigers, and wolves were tanned (preserved) and used for this purpose and to furnish cave dwellings. American Indians, used the preserved heads of porcupines, foxes, raccoons, and eagles to decorate their clothing and equipment; many were preserved in a way that made them look quite natural and lifelike.

Taxidermy, as we know it today, can be traced back only about 400 years when the first attempt on record was the preservation of birds in Holland. As reported, a wealthy Hollander had an aviary of exotic birds brought back from the East Indies. Due to the neglect of a keeper, all the birds died of suffocation; but as the owner wished to keep the skins and plumage for display, they were preserved. The birds were skinned, and the skins were then preserved with several kinds of spices brought to Holland, also from the Indies. The skins were then wired, stuffed—no doubt with cotton or tow—and posed in somewhat of a natural position.

The only written report of the practice of taxidermy concerned the specimens that decorated the rooms of astrologers and apothecary shops in the middle ages and the trophies of the hunt, such as the head and horns of stags, that adorned the halls of the rulers of the land in olden times. One of the first published works on taxidermy is in *Natural History,* published by the Royal Academy of Vienna in 1687. This is a treatise on the dissection of birds and animals. In this work mention is made of Hollanders who were the first to bring into Europe live birds secured on the first voyage to the Indian archipelgo in 1517. No doubt these were the same birds that were "stuffed" in Holland later. Some references give as the oldest mounted museum specimen a rhinocerous in the Royal Museum of Vertebrates, Florence, Italy, about 1500. One can only guess at the methods used in both the preservation of the skin and the mounting. It is likely that the skull and leg bones were used and set up onto a wood armature, and then stuffed. Another specimen is in the Museum at St. Gall, Switzerland—a mounted crocodile 10 to 12 feet in length from Egypt; it has been on exhibit since 1627. The specimen is not kept under glass, which demonstrates how well it has been preserved. Other early books published on the subject, such as R.A.F. Reaumur's *Treatise* (1749), and the guides and pamphlets on the collecting and preserving of natural history specimens, such as those of E. Donovan, W. Swainson, Capt. Thomas Brown, and many others are quite out of date and interesting only from an historical point of view.

One of the earliest big mammal taxidermy mounts there is positive evidence of how mounted was discovered in the early

Muskrat Group: Supposedly the first museum habitat group exhibiting animals, painted background, and natural habitat. Prepared by Carl Akeley, 1890, for the Milwaukee Public Museum. [Milwaukee Public Museum photo.]

1900's, in 1903 to be exact. After the Chicago World's Fair of 1893, the Field Columbian Museum (later the Field Museum of Natural History) acquired many zoological specimens. Among the hundreds of specimens were two adult Gayals and a Sumatran rhinocerous, all mounted somewhere in Europe in the 1800s. In preparing these specimens for exhibition in the museum, it was found that all three animals had been filled with *gravel*.*

Both the French and Germans excelled in the practice of taxidermy in early times and prior to the Great Exhibition, London, 1851; but in later years the English were far superior in their methods. In the late 1800s the Rowland Ward studio was founded in London; the men who first worked at Ward's are credited with many improved methods in taxidermy. It was at Ward's that the *Lion and Tiger* struggle (unnatural natural history) was designed and mounted, then considered the finest animal exhibit of ancient or modern times. Later another animal group, different in design,

* A Taxidermists Sketch Book, Leon L. Pray, (1974): order from Jos. E. Bruchac, Greenfield Center, N. Y.

was mounted by a French taxidermist by the name of Jules Ver-
ieaux. This was titled *The Courier* showing the figure of an Arab (no
doubt modeled in wax) seated upon a camel, the two being attacked
by two lions. This group was first exhibited at the Paris Fair of 1867
and won a gold medal. Later it was purchased by the American
Museum of Natural History; today it is on exhibit at the Carnegie
Museum.

Another outstanding animal group of the day was titled *A
Fight in the Tree Tops,* mounted by William T. Hornaday, one of
America's outstanding taxidermists and a man who did much to
bring the art of taxidermy to the attention of the public. His group
showed two orangutans struggling in the top of a tree; the
branches were of natural wood, the leaves artificial, possibly cast in
wax. This group won a silver medal as the best of show in the First
Annual Exhibition of the Society of American Taxidermists.
Natural grasses, rocks, earth, and small trees came into use about
the middle 1800s, being placed in both small and the larger
museum habitat groups to help convey the feeling of the out-of-
doors.

In early times taxidermy was carried on by a comparatively
small number of people, who were more or less secretive about
their methods; as a result the techniques and methods were very
little known. Later, the demand from museums for highly skilled
taxidermists, coupled with the publication of books and pamphlets
on the subject, had the effect of alleviating this traditional secrecy.

Present-day taxidermy began in the United States in 1861
when Ward's Natural Science Establishment was founded in
Rochester, New York. This institution turned out many famous
taxidermists and preparators such as William T. Hornaday, Fred-
eric S. Webster, John Martens, Joseph Palmer, William J. Critchley,
Thomas W. Fraine, and J.F.D. Bailey. It is to all these men that credit
must be given for the modern methods in use today in taxidermy.
Many of these newer methods were developed and worked out at
Ward's in the next few years by these men and others; all are well
known and have works still on exhibit in many museums today.
Hornaday and Carl E. Akeley worked out newer methods in
taxidermy that revolutionized the art—from "stuffing" to sculptur-
ing the anatomy of the animal. From that day on other methods
were developed by both museum and commercial taxidermists in
all branches of the art, until today the United States leads the world
in true-to-life mounts and habitat groups.

Associated with the beginnings of taxidermy in this country is one Scudder, the founder and proprietor of a small museum in the old alms-house, then in City Hall park in New York City. This museum was later to be acquired by Peale, who owned museums in Philadelphia, and later became the foundation of the famous Peale's Museum of New York.

On March 24, 1880, the Society of American Taxidermists was founded, the first organization of its kind. Three competive and general exhibitions were held: Rochester, December 14–18, 1880; Boston, December 14–21, 1881; and New York City, April 30–May 5, 1883. The Society, founded by America's outstanding taxidermists of the day, presented to the public the "art of taxidermy" as practiced at that time. Methods, no longer secret, were freely discussed, which served to bring about a much higher standard of commercial work and museum exhibits; the "stuffing" of animals was transformed into an elaborate art form.

In 1972, the National Taxidermists Association was founded to carry on the work and to advance the art of taxidermy. This Association follows, in some respects, the Society of American Taxidermists of 1880. The work of many members working today as commercial and museum taxidermists is so advanced that it is impossible to predict what improvements can be made in the future. The following remark is typical: "If we could only make them breathe."

2 | TOOLS, MATERIALS, SUPPLIERS

The tools and materials one must have to practice taxidermy are few; most can be purchased locally. There are a few specialized tools necessary. Below you will find a list of companies specializing in taxidermy supplies. With specially designed tools, work is more easily performed, but it is not important that you have a large number of fine tools to do the job; experience and familiarity with the subject to be mounted are more important. Initially, it is more desirable to spend time in the out-of-doors studying wild-life. Without knowing how birds and animals look alive, you will never excell in taxidermy no matter how versed you are technically.

Invest in good tools; they will do the job and last much longer than cheap ones. Some specialized tool will be expensive, some can be purchased under another name and used for your work although not so designed, and some can be made by a good craftsman. For example, a grapefruit knife, which can be purchased from any variety store, makes an excellent tool for scraping off fat and tissue from the skins of birds and small animals.

As to materials, today it is much cheaper and easier to purchase manufactured materials (such as papier-mâché compound) formulated for such work than to bother mixing from different ingredients. Given in Chapter 3 are formulas for all such materials needed, should you choose to mix them yourself. Always use care in the mixing of ingredients and follow those formulas that have been tested.

As you master the techniques of taxidermy, you may want to add other tools, possibly to substitute for those listed; or you may be able to design a better tool for some special type of work. The following list is given only as a guide to the tools and materials you should have to begin work, and is not intended to be a complete list. As you progress in taxidermy, other tools will be needed for your particular style of working.

Skinning knives
Small surgeon's scalpel
Medium-sized scalpel
Kitchen paring knives, 2 different sizes
Grapefruit knives, 2 different sizes
Butcher's skinning knife
Heavy surgeon's bone cutters
Medium-sized carborundum stone

Forceps
Straight forceps, 4-inch with fine tips
Straight forceps, 6-inch with curved tips
Curved forceps, 8-inch with blunt tips
Curved forceps, 10-inch with blunt tips

Miscellaneous
Small surgical scissors, with straight blade
Large surgical scissors, with one blunt blade
Package of assorted sewing needles, good grade
Tape measure, linen
Box of insect pins (for pinning out specimens)
Package of curved needles, 3-cornered, assorted sizes
Tooth brushes (2), soft bristles, different sizes
Modeling tools (3), assorted sizes
Spatula, medium
Coarse furrier's comb
Double boiler, 1-quart size
Set of artist's oil colors (aerosol paint cans/varnish)
Set of artist's brushes, assorted sizes
Tools (hammers, saws, files, shears, pliers, wood rasps, etc., etc., all of which may be found in most home tool boxes)

Materials
Wood-wool, or excelsior, both fine and coarse grade
Tow, fine grade
Cotton batting, long-fiber grade
Adsorbent cotton
Jewler's cotton
Balsa wood, blocks, assorted sizes
Styrafoam, assorted blocks
Powdered borax (20-Mule Team brand)

White cornmeal
Plaster-of-Paris, Hydrocal grade
Salt, medium and coarse grade
Carpenter's glue
Modeling clay
Petroleum wax, yellow
Sulphonated neat's-foot oil
Cheesecloth, coarse grade
Annealed wire, galvanized, assorted sizes and lengths
Hardware cloth (netting), $\frac{1}{2}$–$\frac{1}{4}$-inch mesh
Glass eyes: best grade manufactured for the taxidermist trade (do not use cheap eyes)
Cotton and linen thread, assorted sizes
Ball, or store twine
Cotton cops (for winding plumage)
Notebook, crayons, pencils

Taxidermy supply companies

Jonas Bros. Inc., 1037 Broadway, Denver, CO. 80203
Elwood Supply Co., 1202 Harney Street, Omaha, NE. 68102
Van Dyke's, Woonsocket, 20, SO. DA. 57385
Clearfield Taxidermy, 603-605 Hannak Street, Clearfield, PA. 16830
Mackrell Taxidermy, Inc., Condordville, PA. 19331
Dan Chase Taxidermy Supply Co., Rt. 2, Box 317, Baker, LA. 70714
Nippon Panel Co., 124 Reynolds Street, South Williamsport, PA. 17701
Colorado Fur Tanning & Fur Dressing Co., 1787 So. Broadway, Denver. CO. 80223
New Method Fur Dressing Co., 131 Beacon Street, So. San Francisco, CA. 94080
The Tannery, Inc., 115 E. Washington St., Lander, WY. 82520

3 | FORMULAS

Nearly all materials and chemicals given here for the different formulas can be purchased from local drug and department stores, or taxidermy supply houses. Substitutions should never be made when buying and mixing the solutions. In Formula #104, two versions are given: one with borax and one with sodium arsenite. There has been much controversy over past years as to which one is best; both have been used with good results. But it must be remembered that the sodium arsenite formula is a deadly POISON; however, if it is *prepared and used with extreme caution,* I can see no danger.

In the chapters that follow the formulas needed will be found listed under the assigned numbers.

#101, Carbolic-acid solution
Water, 1 gallon
Carbolic acid, 1½ tablespoons
Use carbolic-acid crystals and dissolve according to directions on label. Mix solution only as needed.

#102, Preserving solution
Water, 15 parts
Commercial formaldehyde, 1 part
Use only commercial formaldehyde (40%). Mix with water in given ratio. Keep solution tightly closed in container.

#103, Degreasing solution
White gasoline, 8 parts
Commercial alcohol, 2 parts
Mix together; use outdoors, or in a well ventilated place, never near a flame. *Do not leave* uncovered. After use pour off the clear solution from grease that has settled in the bottom of the container.

#104, Preserving solution (Pray)

Water, 1 gallon

Powdered borax, 4 ounces

Formaldehyde (40%), 25 drops (only)

Bring water to boil, allow to cool while adding borax and formaldehyde. Stir until borax is dissolved; a saturate solution is desired. This solution for birds and small animals.

Preserving solution

Water, 1 gallon

Sodium arsenite, 1 ounce

Bring water to boil, allow to cool while adding sodium arsenite. Stir thoroughly until all is dissolved. Keep in *glass* container. Label— POISON; handle with extreme caution.

#105 Body paste

Dextrin, 5 pounds

Glycerine, 6 ounces

Carbolic acid, 2 teaspoons

Borax or arsenic water 2 tablespoons

Use a 2 to 3-gallon crock for mixing. Bring water to a boil. Pour about 2 inches boiling water into the crock, then add the glycerine, carbolic acid, and borax or arsenic water and mix well. Add dextrin, a little at a time, stirring mixture until smooth. Add more of the boiling water, mixing gradually until the solution is the consistency of thin glue. *Note:* use only British Standard Gum Dextrin, #160.

#106, Modeling composition

See Formula #105.

To body paste, add ground asbestos, whiting, or other similar fiber. Work this into the paste a little at a time. Consistency of composition can be controlled by the amount of fiber added.

#107, Modeling wax

Beeswax, 3 parts

Rosin, 1 part

Use only pure white beeswax. Melt both in separate containers in a water bath. Mix together while in a liquid state, then pour into small molds to cool.

#108, Oiling solution

Turpentine, 3 parts

Linseed oil, 1 part

Mix together. Shake well to mix each time used.

#109, Alum-water solution

Water, 1 gallon

Alum, 1 teaspoon

Mix water and alum together, stirring until all alum is dissolved. Only mix enough solution for each job as needed.

#110, Flexible glue

Glue (flake), 9 parts

Glycerine, 1 part

Melt glue in a water bath, having it very thin. Add glycerine mixing thoroughly. Stir well each time used, after melting.

#111, Pickle solution

Water, 1 gallon

Salt, $\frac{1}{2}$ pound

Sulphuric acid, $1\frac{1}{2}$ ounces

Add salt to warm water and stir until thoroughly dissolved; then add sulphuric acid. Allow solution to cool. Keep in wood, or glass container—*never* in metal.

#112, Sulphonated neat's-foot oil solution

Water, 1 part

Sulphonated neat's-foot oil, 1 part

Add the oil to warm water and mix thoroughly. Warm solution each time used.

#113, Alum solution

Water, 1 gallon

Salt, $\frac{1}{2}$ pound

Alum, $\frac{1}{4}$ pound

Carbolic acid, $\frac{1}{2}$ ounce

Add carbolic acid to warm water and mix well. Add other ingredients and stir thoroughly. Solution can be used over and over by the addition of a small amount of salt and alum each time.

#114, Dehairing solution

Water, 1 gallon

Hydrated lime, $\frac{1}{4}$ pound

Red arsenic, pinch

Mix lime and arsenic together with a small amount of water to form a paste. Add this to water, mixing thoroughly. Make enough of the solution to cover the skin. *Note:* this solution is POISONOUS: label it so.

#115, Neutralizing solution

Water, 1 gallon
Boric acid, 1 ounce
Add boric acid to warm water and stir until dissolved. Mix as desired in quanity for use.

#116, Limewater solution

Water, 1 gallon
Slaked lime, 3 ounces
Warm water; add lime and mix thoroughly until dissolved.

#117, Alum salt solution

Water, 1 gallon
Salt, 3 ounces
Chrome alum, 15 grams
Add salt to warm water; mix. Add alum and stir until dissolved. Keep in glass container.

4 | BIRDS

Most beginners in the art of taxidermy start their hobby, or later profession in the mounting of birds. All legally collected birds (sparrows, starlings, crows, etc.) are specimens that can be used for practice by the beginner; later, game birds brought in by the sportsman for mounting. Today, more birds than animals are mounted, but the "know how" in taxidermy is needed and not the methods. A knowledge of the habits and attitudes birds assume in the wild is *most important,* so observe and study birds in their natural habitat and note their many different characteristics. Note how the neck and head come from the body; how the wings are anchored; how the angle of the legs are attached to the body in different attitudes. If bird mounting is to be your first attempt at taxidermy, remember—practice makes perfect, or nearly so!

Feathers of birds are in given areas over the skin, not over the entire body, as is the hair in mammals; these are known as "feather

Eastern Chinese Ring-Neck Pheasant (North America): Mounted by the author from fresh skins.

tracts" as shown (Figs, 1–3). Although feathers are in tracts, it is the down under the feathers that gives the appearance the feathers are located all over the skin. After skinning a bird, removing/scraping the feather butts to remove the fat and inner skin muscles found between each butt is *most important*. If you are to end up with a good mount and one that will keep its shape in years to come, these feather butts must be thoroughly cleaned. Figures 4 and 5 show the skeleton of a bird, and Figure 6 shows the dorsal tract along the back and the names of the feathers.

With some birds it is nearly impossible (unless you are a trained scientist) to determine the sex of many large or small birds prior to skinning, but this can be told from the gonads (Fig. 7).: the testes of the male (*A*) and the ovaries, or egg sac, of the female (*B*).

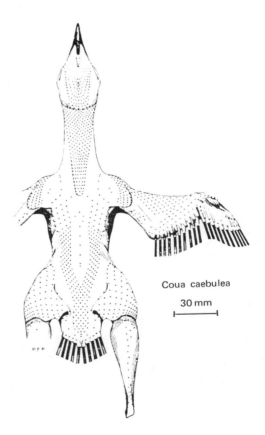

Coua caebulea

30 mm

Fig. 1

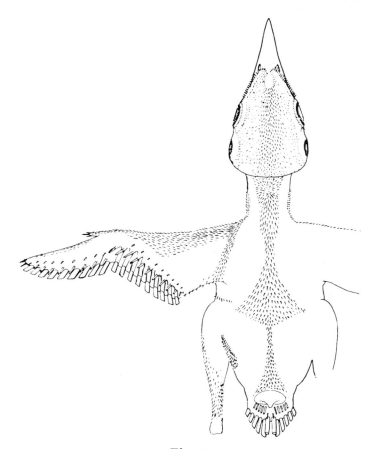

Fig. 2

In the breeding season and in older birds these are more pro-
nounced.

Two birds, a starling (not protected) and wood duck (a game
bird), are used as models in bird taxidermy, but each is skinned and
the skin prepared for mounting in a slightly different manner. The
starling has a tough skin, to which the feathers are firmly attached
(this presents a problem in some other birds). The neck skin can be
inverted over the skull. The wood duck has a thin skin; and, if
healthy, it is fat and greasy. The neck skin cannot be inverted over
the skull. To remove and clean the head the skin will have to be
opened on the neck. This will all be explained later.

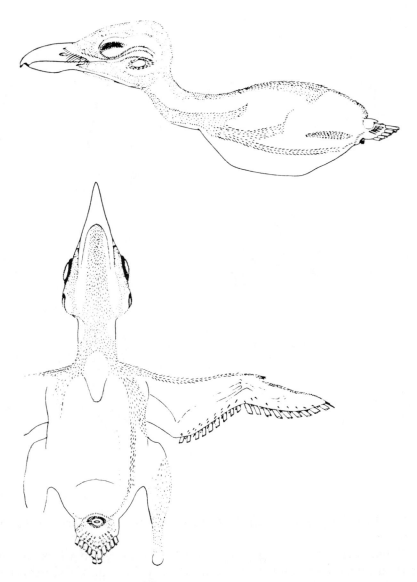

Fig. 3

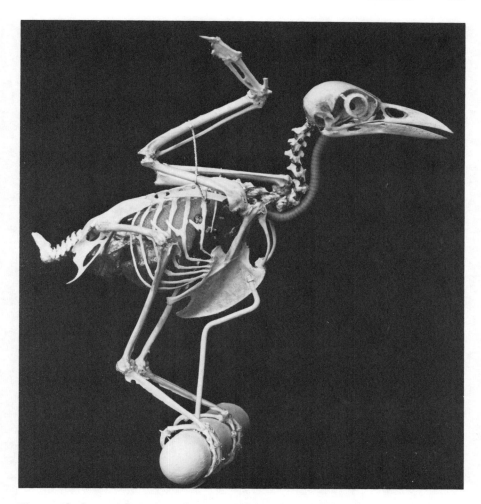

Fig. 4. Skeleton of a crow, showing where the neck, wings, and tail wires should be anchored in the artificial body.

As soon as the specimen is collected, plug up the mouth, nostrils, and all shot holes with cotton. Wash off all blood and body juices with cold water. Take accurate color notes of the eye colors; also, the diameter of the eyes and colors of the bill, legs, and feet of all larger birds with fleshy parts. These notes can be made with crayon pencil if in the field, or by written notes if you are acquainted with colors. If any feathers come out, especially tail feathers, save them, as they can be put back later. Make a cone of newspaper, smooth out the feathers (do not use newspaper if the bird is

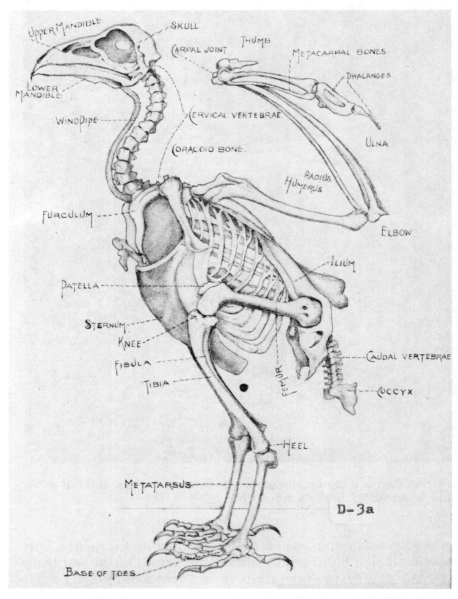

Fig. 5. Skeleton of an eagle. All important bones are indicated.

18

Fig. 6. Main feather tracts and names of feathers.

white or the ink may come off on the feathers), and place the bird, head first, into the cone. This will keep all feathers in place until you are ready to skin. Do not delay skinning longer than necessary, or the bird will spoil. Should you be faced with a delay, place the specimen in a plastic bag, seal (along with the data when collected), and freeze. When ready to skin, defrost slowly in the refrigerator; *do not* thaw quickly as this may cause the feathers to slip. If at all possible skin the bird soon after collecting; mounting can come later.

It is also helpful in the beginning of bird taxidermy (and later if one is truely interested in becoming proficient in the art), to make a contact outline of the bird prior to skinning. Study the specimen and choose the pose you want in the mount; then lay out on a piece of paper and outline in pencil the bird in this position. This contact outline will prove valuable in the shaping/positioning of the bird

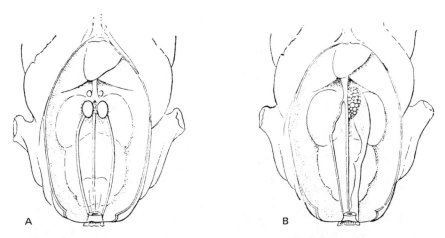

Fig. 7. The sex of many birds can be determined by the gonads: the testes of the male (A) and the ovaries of the female (B).

later. One should also become acquainted with the names of the feathers and the skeleton (bones) of birds, all of which will be helpful later in posing the bird and adjusting the feather pattern. Note where wings and legs come from the body when you pose the bird in different positions—standing, walking, running, and so on. In bird mounting the only bones retained with the skin are the skull, wing bones (in small birds the humerus can be discarded), and the leg bones (in birds such as hawks, herons, etc.) keep the femur bone for a better mount. Before skinning replace all cotton in the throat, shot holes, and eyes. If the eyeball was ruptured when the bird was collected, remove and replace with cotton. Prior to skinning make certain that all feathers/plumage is free of dirt and blood. To end up with a lifelike mount, the specimen must be in good condition for skinning; much time, effort, and disappointment can be avoided if you select as perfect a specimen as possible for your first attempt at bird taxidermy.

SKINNING

On your work table lay the specimen on its back and part the feathers along the bare area down the breast bone. The opening incision/cut is made from a point at the forward tip of the breast bone to the vent; cut through the first ring of the vent muscle, not entirely through the vent. This incision/cut is illustrated in Figure 8

(A–A) and Figure 9 (A–A). Use a sharp scalpel and avoid cutting through and into the abdominal wall, or blood and body juices will run out and damage the feathers. As soon as the opening incision/ cut is made, sprinkle on plenty of powdered borax to absorb the juices and to preserve the skin. Throughout the skinning operation *use plenty of borax*. (Note: if the body is wanted for food, use corn meal instead of borax). If the bird has been shot up and there is spoilage to parts of the skin, mix *1 part alum to 4 parts borax* and use this in the skinning. Work the skin down each side of the body with the fingers; in large birds separate skin and muscles with both fingers and scalpel. When the legs are reached, grasp the leg from outside the skin and force upward over the knee, which exposes the knee joint, and detach with the bone cutters [see Fig. 10 (B) and Fig. 9 (B)]. On mounted birds where the knee is shown (hawks, owls, herons, etc.), the femur bone is best used and is cut away from the body at this time [Fig. 11 (B)]. Do both legs in the same manner.

Work the skin down each side of the body again with the fingers and scalpel to the tail. Be careful in severing the tail from the body or the tail feathers will fall out. Place the bird on its breast with the tail up and bent back. Work the skin from around the rump and cut away from the tail, leaving the tail bone attached to the skin (this can later be cut away). At this point use care not to cut into or

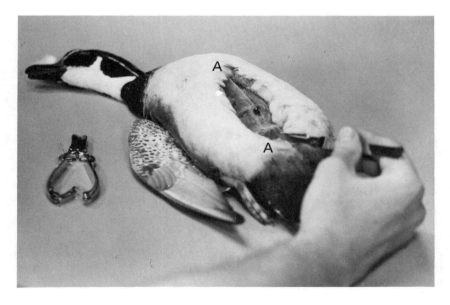

Fig. 8. Opening incision (A–A) tip of breastbone to vent.

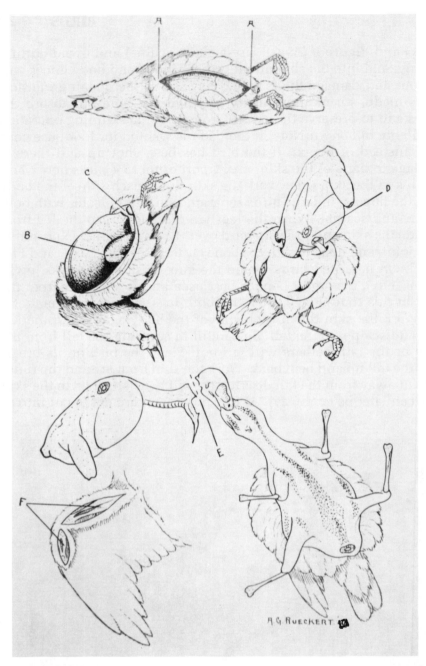

Fig. 9. Opening incision $(A-A)$. Legs disjointed (B); tail cut away (C). Wings disjointed (D). Neck cut away from skull (E). Wings cut open (under side) (F).

22

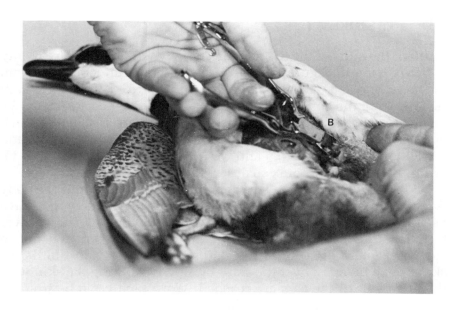

Fig. 10. Detach legs at knee joints (*B*) (some birds).

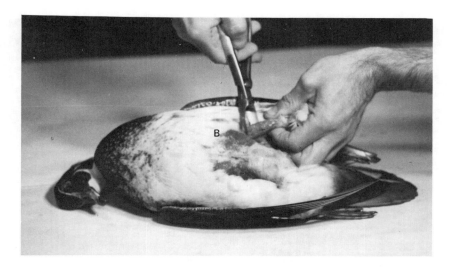

Fig. 11. Detach legs with femur attached (*B*) (other birds).

through the butts of the tail feathers, or they will fall out. *Use plenty of borax here.* In Figure 12 (B–B), the leg bones are cut away from the body, and at (C–C) the tail is severed. Figure 9 (C) shows the tail severed from the body. Work the skin down over the back using the fingers as much as possible until the wings are reached. Detach both from the body by cutting the tendons loose at the ball and socket joint [see Fig. 13 (D) and Fig. 9 (D)]. Do not stretch the skin; again, use plenty of borax to absorb the blood and body juices.

Flesh and muscles on legs and wings can be left until the body is removed, or you can cut away as you skin. After both wings have been detached from the body, work the skin carefully down over the neck (use care in this part of the skinning operation not to stretch the neck skin) until the skull is reached. In most birds the skin can be inverted over the skull by slowly working the skin with the fingers until the ears are reached. Work each ear tube from its socket with the fingers, and when the eyes are reached again use care. Note as you come to the eyes that a transparent membrane covers the eyes; cut this membrane carefully close to the skull so that you do not cut through the eyelids. Continue to skin down to the bill, but do not detach the skin from the bill. The neck and body

Fig. 12. Leg bones (B) and tail (C) detached from body.

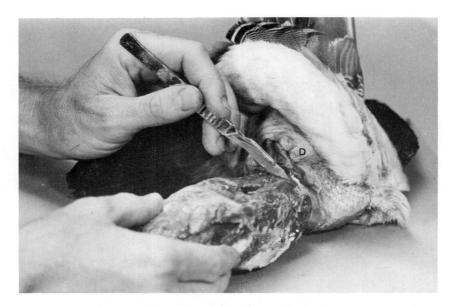

Fig. 13. Wings detached from body at ball-and-socket joint (D).

are now cut from the skull at the base where the neck vertebrae join the skull. Figure 9 shows the skin turned inside out, leg and wing bones cleaned, and neck is detached from the skull (E). In some other birds (ducks, geese, hawks, etc.) the skull is too large to invert the neck skin over, so the skull will have to be removed by an incision/cut either along the top of the skull or on the throat. Figure 14 shows the skin turned inside out (neck and head still attached), with the leg and wing bones cleaned of flesh. Figure 15 illustrates the incision/cut on large-headed birds along the throat. These two incisions/cuts are also shown [Fig. 16 (A–B) and Fig. 17 (A–B)]. To clean the skull, cut away the tongue from inside the mouth, remove the eyes from their sockets, and enlarge the opening in back of the skull only enough to remove the brain. Cut away the muscles of the cheeks and all flesh, but do not disjoint the lower jaws from the skull. *Note:* in hawks, keep the bone and membrane that extends over the eyes that is attached to the skull; in owls, keep the eye bone, removing the eyes from this bone, but use care and do not let the eye fluids run out on to the feathers of the face. This method in both species of birds helps to give a hawklike and owllike expression to the face in the mounted bird (Fig. 18).

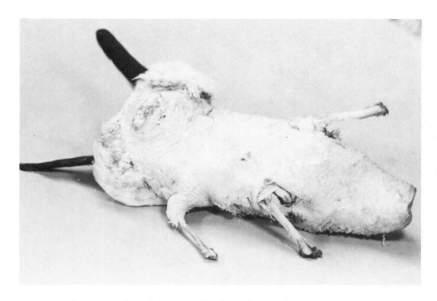

Fig. 14. Skin turned inside out; flesh of leg and wing bones cut away. The neck and head are still with the body skin.

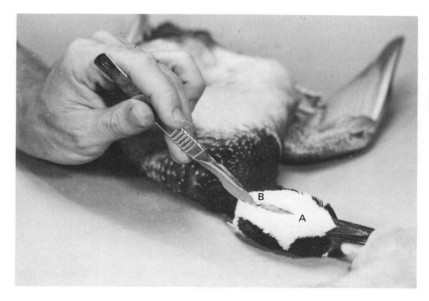

Fig. 15. Opening incision. head (A−B); throat method.

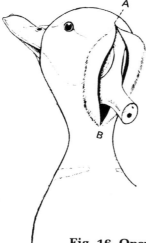

Fig. 16. Opening incision, head (A−B); top of head method.

As soon as the body is removed, turn back the neck skin and smooth out the feathers. In skinning birds use care not to stretch the skin, especially the neck skin or it will be impossible to adjust to a natural pose in the mounted bird. Before turning your attention to the skin, an outline of the body should be made, but first wrap the skin in a cloth dampened with the carbolic-acid-water solution (Formula #101). The body outline and measurements, which should also be made at this time, will be helpful in building the artificial body. Figure 19 shows the outline of the body of the wood duck. It is also helpful to mark on this outline where the wings and legs are to be anchored to the artificial body.

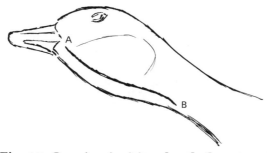

Fig. 17. Opening incision, head; throat method.

Fig. 18. Eye sockets—owls, hawks; leave in skull.

If the flesh and muscles have been removed from the legs and wing bones when skinning, then this part of the operation is over; but, if not, this must now be done. The undersides of the wings are opened as shown in Figure 9 (F), unless the bird is to be mounted in a flying position. Figure 20 (A—B) shows the flesh and muscles that must be removed. In mounting a bird flying, the flesh and muscles

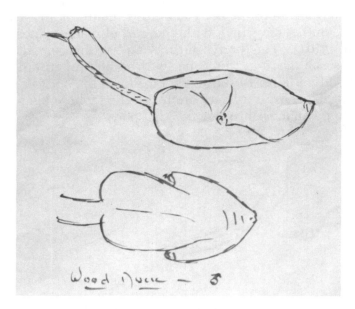

Fig. 19. Outline: wood duck body.

Fig. 20. Opening incision, wings (*A*−*B*); close wing mount.

must be removed from inside the skin. This is a trying job, as you must be careful not to cut away the feathers from the wing bones. If care is used, in some bird mounts the flesh/muscles can be removed as shown; the incision/cut is then carefully stitched together with very fine stitches so they do not show. Do not cut away the feather butts from the bones. In larger birds (and most small ones) remove

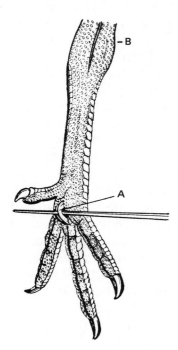

Fig. 21. Removing tendons from legs and toes (*A*); opening leg incision on large birds (*B*).

the tendons in the legs; this is a "must" with all large birds. Cut open along the toes and the pad at the bottom of each foot, and with a sharp pointed tool (awl, forceps, etc.) reach in and pull away the tendons, which appear as strong plastic cords. Figure 21 (A) shows the initial steps in removing a leg tendon. In birds (hawks, owls, pelicans, etc.) it is best to make an incision/cut on the inside of the legs and remove the tendons and flesh through this cut [Fig. 21 (B)]. This cut can later be sewn together with very small stitches. When finishing the mount, use wax to model the leg scales cut. Rub borax into the opening; and to further moth-proof, it is best to inject preserving solution (Formula #104) up inside the legs from where the tendons were removed; be sure to get in enough of this solution.

PREPARING THE SKIN

Most taxidermists mount birds while the skin is still fresh and relaxed, and many fine mounts are the result of this method. I have always had better results by allowing the bird skin to dry for several weeks or months after it has been skinned and cleaned. After the skull is cleaned, cotton is placed in the eye sockets, prior to turning back the skin over the skull, and the body filled out with cotton, or loose tow. It is also helpful to wrap loose cotton around the leg and wing bones before allowing the skin to dry if you do not mount the bird soon after collecting. By allowing the skin to dry for some time, you will find that the mounted bird will hold its pose much better: the borax used in skinning tends not only to preserve but also to leather the skin in much the same manner that leathering/tanning is done to mammal skins. Also, there is not as much shrinkage as in a fresh bird mounted as soon as the specimen was skinned and poisoned. With either technique, the skin must be cleaned of all flesh/muscles and the feather tracts (base of the feathers) scraped and separated. If you have allowed the skin to dry, it can now be relaxed by wrapping the legs in damp cotton (or a cloth for larger birds), the inside of the skin dampened, a damp cloth placed in the body skin and up into the neck, and damp cotton in the eyes and mouth. Dampen all cotton/cloth with the carbolic-acid-water solution (Formula #101). Skins of large birds will have to be kept in a relaxing box (any partly air-tight metal box large enough to receive the bird/s with sand dampened with the solution on the bottom and paper, not newsprint, for the skin/s to lay out on) and the damp cotton/cloth changed until the skin is soft enough to work in removing all flesh, muscles, and fat. Feather tracts and all inner skin must be scraped with a skin scraper, or dull knife, until all flesh particles, inner skin muscles, and all fat is removed and the butts of the feathers separated. Fat birds are difficult to clean, but this fat must be removed or the grease will come out after the bird is mounted and spoil the feathers. Work carefully not to tear the skin; in fat birds this is easily done. Remove the fat around the tail and cut away the fat gland (if this was not done previously) and scrape from tail to head and on each side of the opening incision/cut. Figures 1, 2, and 3 show how the feather tracts of birds are arranged in the skin; it is the base of these tracts that must be cleaned before the bird can be mounted. Use plenty of borax when scraping to absorb the fat and grease; with larger birds and birds with much fat on the inner skin, use coarse sawdust to absorb this fat and grease. Use extreme care not to cut or tear the skin.

Most perching birds are not fat; you will need to clean only the blood, or body juices. This can be done with cotton swabs and water, and dried with a cloth, or a piece of cotton. In fat birds the grease must be removed from the skin if one is to have a mounted bird that will hold its pose and keep the feathers from becoming stained. If the skin is very dirty and greasy, it must first be washed in cold water, into which a very small amount (as per amount of water used) of a mild detergent is mixed; the skin should now be right-side out. Wash the skin thoroughly and immerse several times in clear water to remove all the detergent. Now place the skin with the feathers flat and in order (it will look as though you could never make a good mount from such a skin) between papers, but do not use newsprint if the bird is white, and allow to drain, but not dry. Next, immerse the damp skin in white gasoline and work well with the hands. Very fat birds can stay in the gasoline for several hours, but keep working with the hands in this solution to remove the grease. Remove from the gasoline and drain between papers, or cloth, and allow the paper/cloth to absorb as much of the gasoline as it will; change the papers/cloth several times if necessary.

While the skin is in the gasoline, heat enough plaster-of-Paris to cover the skin. Then place the skin in the warm plaster and work with the hands, making sure the plaster gets to the base of the feathers. Keep working until the feathers appear dry and the down can be "fluffed." The skin can now be removed from the plaster. If compressed air is available, use it to remove the plaster from the skin and feathers. Otherwise you will have to remove the plaster by beating it out with a small, pliable stick such as a piece of thin bamboo. Shake and beat (carefully) until all plaster is out; the plaster *must be removed* from the skin, inside the skin, the feathers, and the down next to the skin. Wrap the legs with a dampened cloth, or cotton, place a damp cloth inside the skin and up into the neck, and insert wet cotton in the eyes and inside the mouth. The skin must be as relaxed and pliable as it was after being skinned before you can attempt to mount the bird.

MOUNTING

If you choose to mount the bird soon after skinning/cleaning, or if you have a dried skin that has been relaxed, both must be free of dirt, blood, body juices, fat, and grease. Only a skin in as perfect condition as you can make it will turn out as a successful mount. Prior to preserving the skin, it is best to make the body, have all wires needed, and to select the perch, or base, for anchoring the specimen. All materials to be used in mounting the bird should be at hand prior to removing the skin from either the freezer or relaxing box. In some birds you will find that the leg or wing bones have become broken, or the skull damaged. All must be repaired before starting to mount the bird. This can be done by the use of a small stick/dowel worked down inside the broken bones where the marrow was removed (the marrow in the bones must be removed, especially in all large birds, by cleaning out with a pipe-stem cleaner, or cotton wrapped around wire). Repairing the bones and skull are illustrated in Figure 22; (1–2–3) shows how the skull can be repaired. In (1) the top of the skull has been fastened together with small wires; in (2) the top of skull has been repaired with papier-mâché, or composition (Formula #106); in (3) the entire skull has been carved from balsa wood; in (4–5–6–7–8) leg and wing bones have been repaired with small sticks/dowel/wires; in (9) the bill (upper mandible) has been repaired with a small wire. Holes in the skin of all large birds should be stitched. Be careful not to pull the skin too tight, or catch the base of the feathers. After all work previously described has been completed, the skin must be preserved. Use either of the preserving solutions (Formula #104) and cover all parts: head, wings, legs, base of the tail, and outside and inside of the legs and feet. To get the solution inside the legs, it may be possible to inject the solution into the channel where the tendons were removed. The skin must be thoroughly moistened.

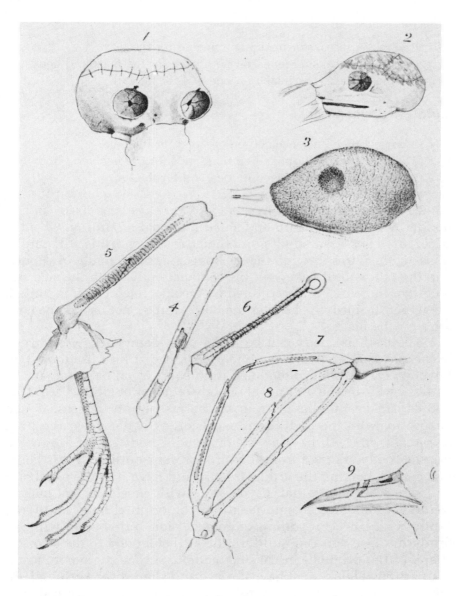

Fig. 22. Methods of repair; skull, leg, wing bones, and bill.

To mount the bird/s you need the artificial body, wires to support the specimen, cotton, tow, and the perch, or base. For the starling, select the following wires:

> #18 wire, 2 pieces, sharpened on one end for the legs
> #20 wire, 1 piece, sharpened on both ends for the neck and body
> #20 wire, 1 piece, sharpened on one end for the tail

and for the wood duck:

> #10 wire, 2 pieces, sharpened on one end for the legs
> #13 wire, 1 piece, sharpened on both ends for the neck and body
> #16 wire, 1 piece, sharpened on one end for the tail

Annealed, galvanized wires should always be used in all taxidermy, especially bird and small mammal mounting. Give the wires more of a squared-off point than a round one; this will help in pushing the wires through the leg bones, the neck, and wing bones, and the tail, and to anchor in the artificial body. Both the size and length of the wire are determined by the specimen being mounted; the larger the bird, the heavier the wires, but do not use too heavy a wire for the neck.

The artificial body can be made from dampened wood wool/ excelsior (used for years by taxidermists and still in use today), or the body carved/shaped/modeled from balsa wood or styrafoam, or bodies cast from the original and made of paper or cloth. These cast bodies can be purchased from taxidermy supply houses. If you choose to wrap the body from excelsior, or better yet carve from styrafoam, you will have a "custom-made" body if you follow the original body skinned from the bird, or your outline of this body. Use care in making the artificial body and have it to the exact size and shape of the original. If you wrap with excelsior, first make a round core about the same length of the original body and wrap firmly with cord. By adding more excelsior to this core, winding firmly in place you can build up the artificial body to the size and shape of the original. In carving/modeling from styrafoam, again your artificial body must have the size and shape of the original. *Do not get the body too large.* If too small one can use loose filling of fine tow or excelsior where needed, but this cannot be done if the body is too large. From your data make the neck from fine tow, or jewelers cotton (used in small birds) by measuring the length of the neck (original), leaving an extra length to anchor in the skull and rub wax on the neck wire; the wax will hold the tow, or cotton, as you build up the artificial neck to its proper size. For a strong neck and one that will help to keep the neck skin relaxed while working, mix a quantity of cold water paste (one trade name, Gumbo), and use this paste from time to time as you build up the neck. This will not only keep the neck skin damp, but as the paste dries it makes a very strong neck, so strong in fact that one can pick up the mounted bird by the head/bill and handle it with no danger that the neck will break away from the body.

After the neck is made, anchor it in to the artificial body in the same position as was the original by running the wire through the body and bending into a U and clinching. Figure 23 shows the original body of the wood duck and the artificial body and neck; the artificial body is carved from styrafoam. Figure 24 shows the artificial body of the starling, carved from balsa wood; (A) shows how the neck and body wire is anchored to the body, and (B) shows the neck wound with fine tow. Note that enough wire has been left to go through the skull and out either the top of the head or the mouth.

The leg wires are run up through the legs from the bottom of the feet—first through the pad of the foot, then up the leg following the channel where the tendons were removed. Use care over the

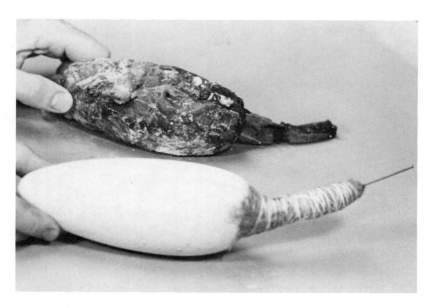

Fig. 23. Natural body (wood duck) and artificial body carved from styrofoam; neck wrapped on wire with fine tow.

Fig. 24. Artificial body and neck; neck wire anchored (*A*); length of neck (wrapped with tow) anchored to body (*B*). Leg bone wrapped with tow (*C*); tail wire (*D*). Artificial neck inside skin (*E*); artificial body inside skin (*F*). Tail anchored to body (*G*); leg anchored to body (*H*); neck

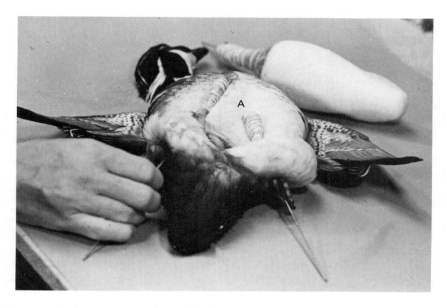

Fig. 25. Flesh cut away from leg bones, replaced with fine tow held in place with string (A).

heel joint so the wire will not come through the leg skin at this point. Then tie the wire loosely to the leg bone. Replace the flesh/ muscles cut away with either fine tow or jewelers cotton, then wrap with fine thread to hold all in place. Figure 25 (A) shows both leg bones wrapped with tow. Figure 24 (C) shows one leg bone wired and cotton wrapped to replace the muscles cut away; at (D) the tail wire is pushed through the tail bone and up into the skin to anchor the body later.

The wings are wired next, and if the mount is to be with closed wings they are wired (in small birds the wings will not have to be wired) as shown in Figure 26. The wing wire run down along the bone, bent in a U shape, and the flesh/muscles are replaced with either fine tow or cotton, depending upon the specimen. If the bird is to be mounted in a flying position the wings are wired with wires of the proper size and length (depending upon the specimen being mounted) and wired from inside the skin (Fig. 27). Run the wires

anchored with wire through skull (I); wing anchored with large pin (J). Mounted bird (starling) on branch/perch; feather pattern held in place with pins and string; bill held together with a pin; toes held to branch with pins (K).

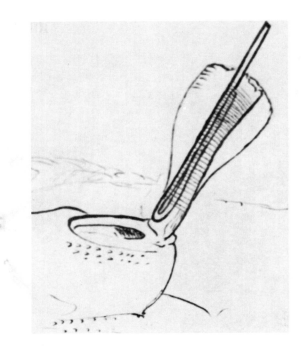

Fig. 26. Wiring wings, to replace flesh; closed wing mount.

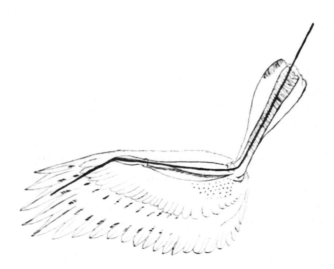

Fig. 27. Wiring wings, to replace flesh; open wing mount.

down the humerus between the ulna and radius and through the wrist (hand) and anchor into the base of the third (primary) feather. Flesh and muscles cut away are replaced with either cotton or fine tow, and the wing wire is left long enough to be anchored into the artificial body. Anchoring the wing wires in their proper position to the body is *most important*. After the legs, wings, and tail are in place, the artificial body with the neck is fitted into the skin. Figure 28 shows the artificial body of the wood duck being adjusted into the skin; Figure 24 (F) shows the artificial body and Figure 24 (E) the artificial neck of the starling. After the neck and body are in place, make certain the body fits, not too large, nor too small. The neck is worked up into the neck skin and into the base of the skull; allow about 1 inch of the neck to fit into the opening in the skull from which the brain was removed. There are two ways to anchor the skull/head; the wire can be run up through and out the top of the skull, or out through the mouth between the upper and lower mandibles. If the bird has a crest, it is best to run the wire through the mouth; use this method also for all birds with a long bill. Figure 29 shows the legs, tail, and neck (head) anchored to the artificial

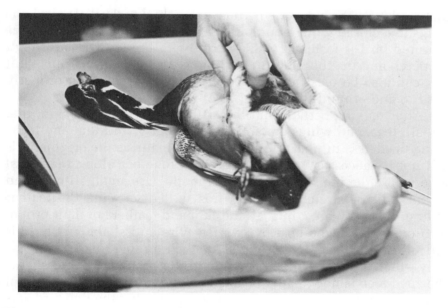

Fig. 28. Inserting artificial body and neck into prepared and poisoned skin.

Fig. 29. Artificial body in skin; neck, legs, and tail have been anchored to body by clinching wires into body.

body. In Figure 24 the tail is anchored to the body (G) the legs are anchored (H), the neck wire runs through the skull (I), and the wings in a closed wing mount are anchored (J). In Figure 24 (K) the mounted bird is fastened to the perch with the leg wires through the perch and the toes held in position with small insect pins. Soft wax can also be used for this, as the feet (toes) must be properly fitted to and around the perch (limb) in a natural position.

After making certain that the artificial body fits the skin, that the tail, legs, and wings are anchored properly, and that any loose filling needed is in place (if the body was made as the original this will not be necessary), the skin is sewn together along the breast bone where the incision/cut was first made. Use small stitches and do not pull or stretch the skin; this will disarrange the feather pattern. After sewing adjust all the skin and feathers in their proper position. Pick up the bird by one leg wire and shake gently; this will allow the feathers to adjust to their proper place over the body—that is, if the body was made to the proper size and shape. The specimen is now ready for the final and most important part of bird taxidermy: to show how well you know what the live bird was like in life and how well you have built the artificial body.

SHAPING THE SPECIMEN

Fasten the bird to its perch or base with the two leg wires running through the legs and out the bottom of the feet. These support wires should be of the proper distance apart that the bird would alight, or stand. Now give the legs their proper angle, bending at the heel just above the tarsus. If you have used the femur bone, adjustments will have to be made to both the femur and heel. Many first faults in bird taxidermy (especially with water birds) is that the legs have been achored too far back on the artificial body; this tends to make the specimen out of balance, the legs coming from the body too close to the tail. After you have anchored the bird in either a perching or standing position, turn your attention to the neck. Bend the neck first where it comes from the body at the breast, then where it enters the base of the skull. At this time you must decide if the bird is to be in an alert pose, or one at rest. Figure 30 shows the wood duck on its perch, head in an alert position, and wings being anchored.

Fig. 30. Adjusting wings; anchoring in position with large pins.

Fig. 31. Wood duck, adjusted/shaped into position; tail spread held in place with strips of cardboard; feet and toes pinned to branch.

Fig. 32. Feathers held in place with cardboard; bill tied together; feet and toes pinned to branch.

Fig. 33. Another method of holding feather pattern in place with string.

Fig. 34. Starlings (winter and summer plumage) mounted by carving, or wrapping body method.

Wings must be in their proper position, high on the body, to give a natural and lifelike look to the mounted bird. If the artificial body has been made correct as to size and shape, you will not have to tie down the feathers. In the wood duck mount (Fig. 31) note that as the artificial body was exact, only the tail feathers are held in position between two pieces of cardboard. In Figure 32 note another position where the feathers have been held in place along the back and sides with cardboard. In Figure 33 it was necessary to hold feathers in this mount with fine thread wrapped around the bird and cardboard. The bird here is on a temporary base. Figure 24 (K) shows the starling on its perch, pins holding the upper and lower mandibiles together and pins holding fine thread wrapped around the bird to keep the feather pattern in place while allowing all to dry. It is also *important* that you check on the mounted bird for the first few days so that any feathers needing additional arranging can be done before the skin sets/dries. Mounted starlings in winter and summer plumage are shown in Figure 34.

Some taxidermists prefer to set the glass eyes while the skin is still relaxed and adjustments are being made in shaping the specimen. This can now be done; or better yet, with some birds—the larger ones—let the specimen dry, then relax the eyelids with the *carbolic-acid-water solution* when the eyes can be set and the lids adjusted. Setting the eyes is most important; they must not be too far in their sockets, nor should they be too far out from the head, a common mistake. The expression of the mounted bird is in the eyes. Papier-mâché, or composition, can be used to set and hold the eyes in their proper place. Allow the specimen to dry thoroughly; this will take several days/weeks depending upon the bird being mounted.

FINISHING

After the specimen has thoroughly dried, remove all cardboard, pins, and thread, and cut protruding wires and the one from the top of the head close to the skull; if neck wire sticks through the mouth, that wire must be cut off when adjusting/shaping the specimen, and at the same time tying the bill together. Now refer to the color notes and restore the colors that have faded to the bill, legs, and feet, also around the eyelids. Do not paint on colors too heavy, or you will end up with a painted look, which should be avoided. Colors in all specimens of taxidermy should have a tinted, not a painted look.

MOUNTING, ANOTHER METHOD

For larger birds and those with long legs, the artificial body can be carved from balsa wood, styrafoam, and/or other types of materials, or the skeleton can be used. In Figure 35 the artificial body (purchased from a taxidermy supply house) of a pheasant is illustrated; the neck wire comes anchored in the body. Also shown is where the tail and legs are to be anchored. In Figure 36 the body has been carved (following the original) of styrafoam, the artificial neck and

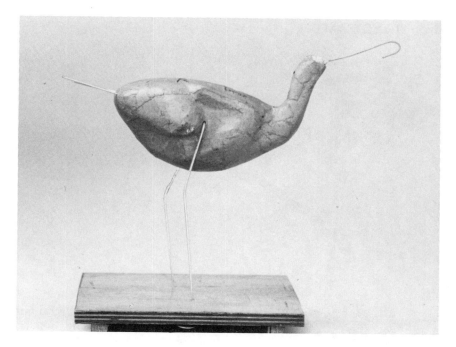

Fig. 35. Artificial body (paper) of a pheasant; neck, tail, and leg wires anchored; purchased from supply house.

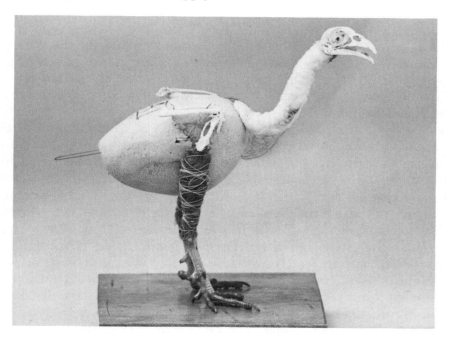

Fig. 36. Study of artificial body of pheasant showing inside of mount with skin and feathers removed; also showing crop.

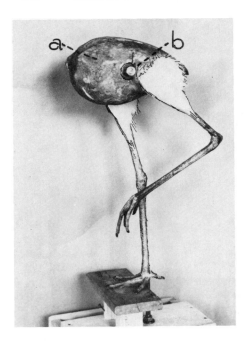

Fig. 37. Large birds; artificial body carved from balsa wood; legs cut from skin, cleaned, then anchored to body by iron rods.

the skull are anchored, the wing bones are in place, the tail wire is anchored to the body, and the legs are wrapped with fine tow, to replace the flesh and muscles cut away. This photo serves as an "inside view" of a pheasant in a standing pose. In Figure 37 the legs have been cut from the skin, wrapped with fine tow, and the body carved from balsa wood. Shown also is where the artificial neck is to be anchored (a) and where the leg bones are anchored to this balsa body (b). The balsa body should be shellacked prior to placing the skin. In Figure 38 is illustrated the skeleton of an osprey cleaned of all flesh, muscles, and so on, poisoned with formaldehyde (full strength) brushed over the skeleton after it has been fastened to the perch or base it is to be mounted upon. Flesh and muscles that were cut away are now reproduced with papier-mâché or composition (Formula #106); and after all has set/dried, the cleaned and preserved skin of the bird is adjusted over the modeled form. Figure 39 shows the form ready to receive the skin, and Figure 40 shows the finished mount of an osprey.

Again, as in all branches of taxidermy, the method/s used in bird taxidermy is not important. What is *most important* is your knowledge of the attitudes birds take on in life and your ability to

Fig. 37a. Whale-Headed Stork (Africa): Main figure in habitat group. Mounted by the author from skin collected for group, using technique described in text. [Field Museum of Natural History photo.]

Fig. 38. Skeleton of an osprey, cleaned, poisoned; body core of balsa wood, neck and leg wires anchored to wood core.

Fig. 39. Anatomy modeled over skeleton with papier-mâché; skeleton acting as framework or armature.

Fig. 40. Mounted osprey, using the technique described in text.

48

Fig. 41. Eagle Owl (Europe): Main figure in habitat group. Mounted by the author from collector's scientific skin and skeleton (see text). [Field Museum of Natural History photo.]

duplicate and build an artificial body as near the original as is possible—then, with the experience you have gained, to adjust/ shape the bird in as lifelike a pose as the bird took on in life and when dry to restore the faded colors.

The bird should be mounted, not "stuffed."

5 | MAMMALS

Mammal taxidermy, like bird taxidermy, is first dependent upon your knowledge of the life-habits of the animal you are to mount, either small or large. You must have field experience in the study of wildlife before you can become a good taxidermist. Anyone can read and follow directions, but after you have the specimen skinned, the artificial body wired, and glass eyes in place, it is observations made in the field of the animals you are about to pose that counts. Techniques and formulas can be learned, but it takes months/years of observing animals in their natural habitats, and then hard work to achieve lifelike positions in your mounted specimens.

Have in mind also the position you want in the finished mount prior to skinning; you will make the opening incision/cut either on the back or belly of the specimen. To illustrate, we use a fox squirrel, as this small mammal has a very tough skin and the species are plentiful in nearly all parts of the country.

PREPARING THE SPECIMEN

For your first specimen select an animal that is in good fur and one not too badly shot up. Wipe off the blood and body juices with cold water and plug up any shot holes with cotton or grasses. It is always helpful, as in bird taxidermy, to make a contact outline of the squirrel (or the animal you are about to mount), in the pose you have in mind before skinning. Lay the specimen out on a plain piece of paper and pose in position, then trace around the body with a pencil, marking in any additional data that will help later. After the animal has been skinned, other measurements can be taken from the body and indicated on your outline.

SKINNING

Lay the squirrel on its back, and with a sharp scalpel or knife make the opening incision/cut from a point between the front legs to a point between the back legs. This is illustrated in Figure 42 (A—B) and Figure 43 (A). At this time it is also advisable to open the bottom of each foot with a small incision/cut [Fig. 43 (A—1)]; this will simplify skinning when you reach the legs/feet. The opening incision/cut is generally made when the specimen is to be mounted in a running, climbing, or similar pose; if the specimen is to be sitting, it is best to make the opening incision/cut down the back, as illustrated in Figure 44 (A—B). By this method it is easier to insert the artificial body, as will be explained later. With either opening, use care not to cut through and into the abdominal wall, or blood and body juices will run out and cause trouble.

Carefully work the skin (you will have to use the scalpel in skinning mammals more than you did with birds) down each side of the body until the legs are reached (Fig. 45). Skin the legs down to the toes; if you have made an incision/cut on the bottom of the feet, this will help as the skin must be worked down to the toes. Separate each toe and cut off the leg and foot, but leave the foot attached to the skin [Fig. 46 (A)]. Figure 43 (B) shows another

Fig. 42. Opening (belly) incision (A—B).

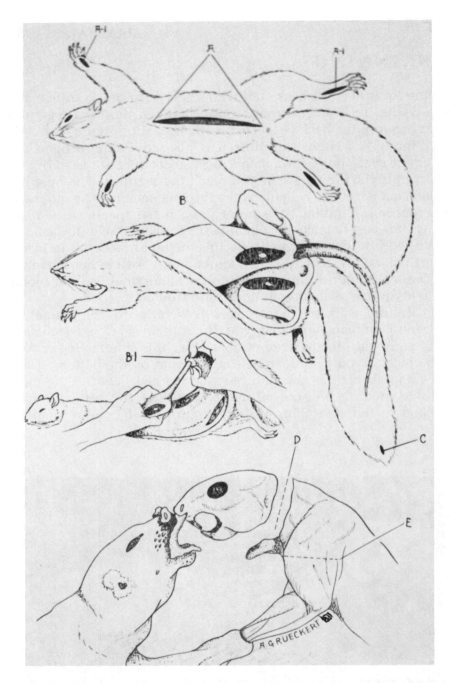

Fig. 43. Opening incision (A); incision on feet (A−1). Leg disjointed from body (B); incision, tip of tail (C). Removing tail from skin (B−1). Disjointing skull from body (D); disjointing front leg from body (E).

52

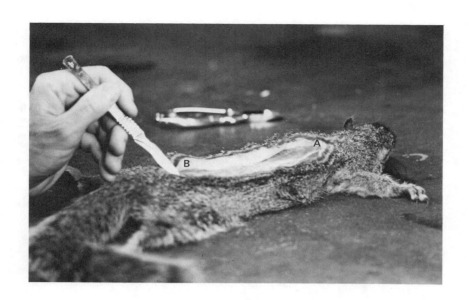

Fig. 44. Opening (back) incision (*A*—*B*).

Fig. 45. Removing skin; work down each side of body.

53

Fig. 46. Disjointing leg (back) (A).

method—to cut away the entire leg from the body, as the leg bones are to be used later in mounting.

After each leg has been skinned out, make a small cut on the underside and approximately an inch from the tip of the tail [Fig. 43 (C)]. Then work the skin from around the butt of the tail by grasping the tail with a heavy pair of forceps, or use your fingers and carefully work the tail from the skin. *Be sure* that all the tail bone comes loose clear to the tip. If any small part of the bone is left in the skin it will cause the hair at the tip of the tail to come out. Figure 47 shows the tail being worked loose with the aid of the forceps, and with the fingers [Fig. 43(B–1)]. In any case, *all the tail bone out.*

Continue working the skin down over the back until the front legs are reached. Skin out both the front legs as was done with the back ones, leaving the feet attached to the skin. You will find that the scalpel must be used throughout the skinning operation. Figure 48 shows one leg skinned out (A) and the other leg skinned out with the foot left in the skin (B). The method whereby the front legs are cut away from the body is shown in Figure 43 (E), as was done with the back legs. Continue to work the skin down over the skull and cut the skin close to the skull with care, especially around the

Fig. 47. Pulling tail/bone from skin.

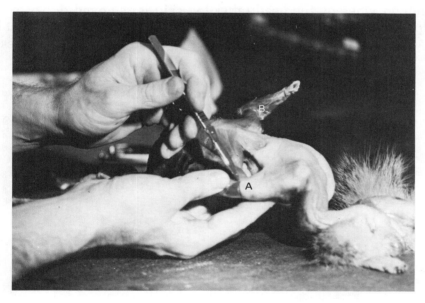

Fig. 48. Skinning front leg (*A*); leg skinned out (*B*).

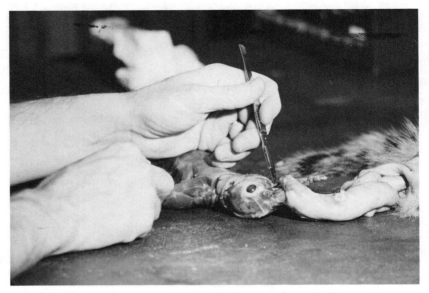

Fig. 49. Skin being removed from body; cut close to lips and nostrils.

ears and eyes. When the lips are reached, skin away from the teeth, but do not cut through the lip skin. Figure 49 shows the skin being worked from around the lips, and Figure 43(D) shows another method whereby the head (after the skin is removed down to the lips) is detached from the body. The head, after cleaning, will be used in a different method of mounting. Cut the end of the nose skin

Fig. 50. Outline of body; skin, cleaned, and poisoned.

close to the skull so the nostrils will remain on the skin. Remove the skin from the body, and at this time make a contact outline of the body with the skin removed. This will be of help later in mounting the squirrel, either by wrapping the artificial body from excelsior or by the more modern method of modeling/carving the body with balsa wood or styrafoam. Measurements of the original body should be taken and indicated on the outline (Fig. 50).

CARE OF THE SKIN

The skin must now be washed in cold, running water to remove all dirt, blood, and body juices. Do this several times until the skin is clean. Next immerse in commercial grain alcohol, which tends to "set" the skin, making it easier to work when mounting. Keep in a glass (not metal) container, and for an animal the size of a squirrel leave in the alcohol over night; soak larger specimens a longer time.

Fig. 51. Outline drawing; anatomy of squirrel.

Keep both the skin and container well covered. Remove from the alcohol and work the skin over the small shaving beam (see, Chapter 8, "Tanning") and with a skin scraper or knife scrape the inner skin to break up the fibers and cut away all inner skin muscles. Shave down around the base of the ears and the eyes and cut away the cartilage from around the nostrils. Carefully split open the lips and cut away the thick flesh of the gums. Remove all flesh from the base of the feet and from between the toes. The skin after cleaning and fleshing is next poisoned by brushing the solution over the inside of the skin; be sure that all parts are well poisoned (Formula #104). You will have to decide which of the two solutions to use. After poisoning, roll up the skin, flesh side in, and lay away until the artificial body is made. Do not let the skin dry out, but keep relaxed until ready to adjust over the body form. If necessary, keep it relaxed by dampening with the carbolic-acid-water solution (Formula #101).

Figure 51 is a drawing of the anatomy of a fox squirrel, showing the muscles of the entire body. This is an excellent study should you want to carve or model an artificial body.

MOUNTING

In former days the mounting of mammals was done by the old "stuffing" method. Today, more modern methods have been worked out whereby the skin is adjusted over an artificial body that has been modeled/carved/cast from the original. These artificial bodies are either purchased from taxidermy supply houses, carved by the taxidermist from balsa wood or styrafoam following the outline made from the original body, or better yet carved while you still have the original body to follow as to measurements and anatomy.

Figure 52 shows the artificial body of a squirrel that has been modeled/cast in styrafoam. It is to be mounted in a sitting pose (other forms can be purchased in different positions). The form must first be smoothed and all rough spots (or where the halves of the mold were cast) trimmed away, as illustrated. Wires to support the mount must be prepared, and for a squirrel you will need

#12 wire, 4 pieces, sharpened on each end for legs
#14 wire, 1 piece, sharpened on each end for head
#18 wire, 1 piece, sharpened on each end for tail

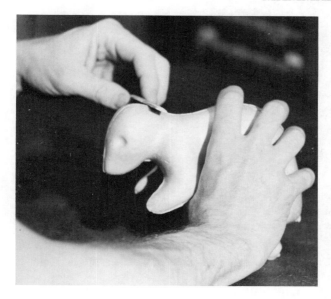

Fig. 52. Removing excess material from halves of form, as cast.

When using a form, you will not need the head wire—the head is cast on the form. Larger animals will need heavier wires to support the specimen.

From your measurements, the artificial tail must be made by rubbing wax along the wire so that jewelers cotton or fine tow will adhere to the wire in building up the tail to the exact length and thickness. In Figure 53 the tail has been anchored to the form in its proper position and glass eyes of the correct size and color have been set in the eye sockets modeled in the form. Wires for the legs and feet are anchored in the form, which is now ready to receive the skin. Figure 54 shows the skin being pulled and adjusted to the form.

Before pushing the leg wires through the bottom of the feet, place a small wad of either papier-mâché or composition (Formula #106) at the base of each foot, then push the wires of the front feet first through the bottom of each foot. The skin can now be pulled over the form; if you have skinned out the body by the back incision/cut, this can be done easily. In Figure 55 the skin has been adjusted over the head, both the front and back legs have been anchored to the form, and the incision/cut along the back is ready to close. Sew with strong thread using small stitches and be careful

Fig. 53. Modeled body form; note wires for legs and wrapped tail wire.

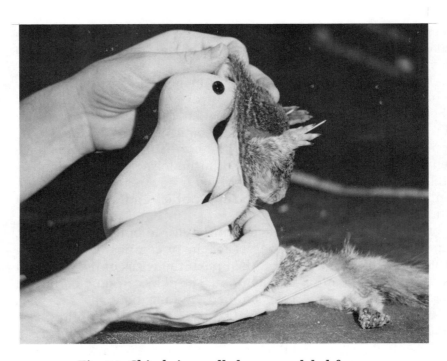

Fig. 54. Skin being pulled over modeled form.

60

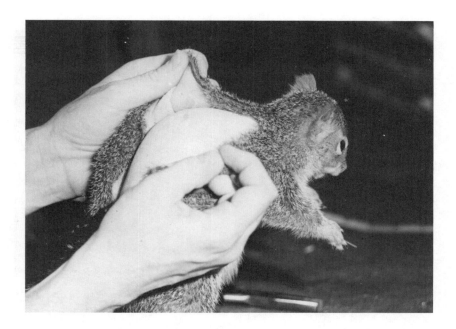

Fig. 55. Skin being adjusted into place.

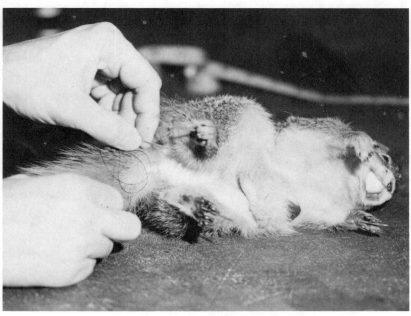

Fig. 56. Sewing (belly) incision.

61

Fig. 57. Placing mount on wood base.

Fig. 58. Pins hold eyes, nostrils, and toes in position until dry.

Fig. 59. Close-up; pins holding eyes and nostrils; note wire mesh holding ears.

not to pull the skin too tight, but be sure the opening is closed. With other mammals, it may be that the opening incision/cut has to be made at the front, or belly, to get the skin in place; if so, this opening can now be sewn together (Fig. 56). It is important to keep the skin relaxed while working as all parts must be adjusted to their proper place over the form. Keep the eyes and lips well relaxed; modeling composition is now worked through the eyelids and lips so as to have a base to model the expression around eyes, lips, and nostrils. In Figure 57 the mount has been fastened to the log base, the tail has been bent into position, and the squirrel is ready for the finishing/shaping. As the form has taken on the position of the mount, this cannot be changed, but the eyes, lips, and nostrils will have to be modeled and the toes of the front and back legs pinned out. In Figure 58 the finishing has been completed, and Figure 59 shows a closeup showing the eyes, lips, and nostrils held in place with insect pins and the ears held in position using cardboard, or small pieces of wire mesh as shown.

ANOTHER METHOD

If one has had some experience in carving, the artificial body can be shaped from balsa wood or styrafoam. Following either the original body, or the contact outline and measurements the body and skull can be carved to size and shape. If the natural skull is to be used, it is cleaned of all flesh; the eyes, brain, and muscles are cut away, poisoned, and the skull is fastened to the carved body.

> **Note:** Placing the skull in boiling water for a time will help in cleaning all flesh, but do not leave too long or the skull (bones) will come apart.

Figure 60 shows an artificial body with the skull carved from balsa wood, and Figure 61 (A) shows the artificial body also carved from balsa wood, but the natural skull has been fastened in position as it is to be used in the mount. In Figure 61 (A–1) the artificial body is carved/shaped so the specimen can be mounted in a sitting position. In this method of mounting the tail wire is wrapped with cotton or fine tow to the proper size and length of the original; Figure 61 (B) and (B–1) show where the tail is to be anchored to the body. The leg bones have been saved, muscles/flesh have been cut away, and the bones have been cleaned. Using fine tow, which is wrapped in place around the bones being held there with thread,

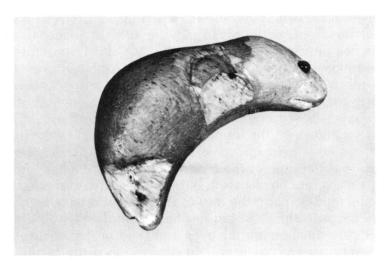

Fig. 60. Carved body (balsa wood) for chipmunk; note skull carved; eyes in place.

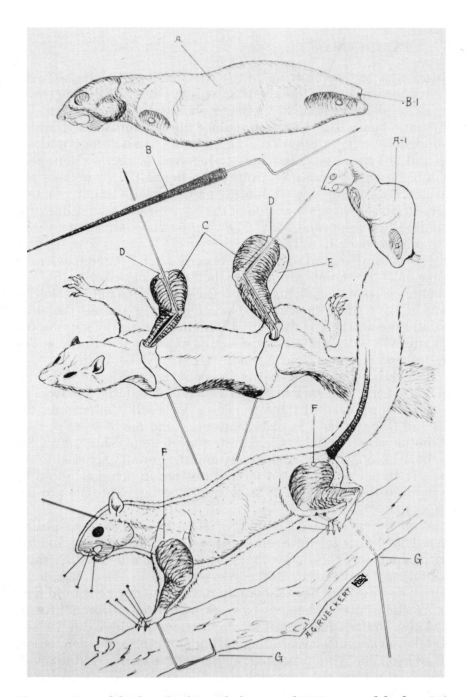

Fig. 61. Carved body, climbing (balsa wood) (*A*); carved body, sitting (*A–1*); where tail fastens to body (*B–1*); tail wrapped on wire (*B*). Fine tow replaces flesh (*C*); wrapped on leg bones (*D*); composition to build out muscles (*E*). Legs anchored to body (*F*); mount fastened to branch (*G*); note pins holding lips and toes in place.

the leg muscles are built up to the exact size and shape as were those of the original before the flesh was cut away. If the leg bones are not used the legs must be made using wires to represent the bones, and again tow is used to replace the flesh/muscles wrapped around the wires. In Figure 62 the body is of balsa wood and the legs and tail are in position ready to receive the skin. In Figure 61 (C) tow has been wrapped around the bones (D) to replace the muscles/flesh of the legs, and at (E) papier-mâché or composition has been placed on the rear side of the back legs to give fullness in modeling the legs to the body. The wrapped legs are shown ready to be pushed back in to the skin.

It is helpful, and in some mounts very much needed if a wad of papier-mâché or composition is pushed down each leg to the foot and at the base of the tail; also where the skull (if the natural skull is used) is fastened to the body. Use composition around the eyes, lips, and the nostrils, as this will fill out any depressions under the skin and will be helpful in modeling the expression of the face. The composition will also hold the skin in place while drying.

The skin, relaxed and poisoned, is now adjusted over the artificial body. Leg wires are run through each foot and the skin worked up and around each of the legs. The skin is adjusted around the eyes and lips and held in place with pins, and the toes are pinned out on the base that holds the mount. Figure 61 (F) shows how the legs have been anchored to the body and the mount anchored to the limb (G). Insect pins are used to hold the toes in position, and pins are holding the lips in place after modeling the expression to the face.

With either method of mounting, after the skin has been pulled and adjusted over the form, and the eyes and lips modeled and the toes pinned out, the hair should be combed and brushed until smooth. Any depressions in the skin—around the face, ears, eyes, nostrils, or feet—that have shown up during the drying should now be corrected. This can be done by working the composition through the skin with the fingers until the depressions are filled out. Drying will take several days/weeks depending upon the specimen, but as it dries keep checking to see that no part of the skin is drying out of shape. Many times such mistakes in the mount can be corrected while the specimen is drying, but not after all has dried and set.

After the specimen has thoroughly dried, remove all pins and wires, and cut off any protruding wires. Brush and comb the hair and "fluff" up the tail (if a squirrel, or similar mount), or better yet keep brushing the tail while the specimen is drying. Some

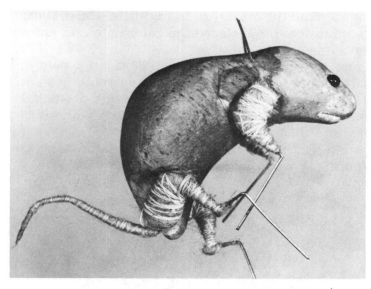

Fig. 62. Body with wired and wrapped legs and tail.

taxidermists cut the tail from the skin, clean and poison, then insert the wrapped tail and keep working the tail hairs to "fluff" while the specimen is drying; later the tail is attached to the mount. One can experiment to find the best method. All traces of papier-mâché or composition is cleaned from around the eyes and lips, and if needed modeling wax (Formula #107) is used to model any

Fig. 63. Mounted chipmunks.

shrinkage around the eyes, lips, and nostrils. The eyelids, lips, and nostrils are restored to their natural color with oils, and the specimen is complete.

Figure 63 shows chipmunks mounted on a natural base; in Figure 64 a mounted fox squirrel is shown entering a nest. In Figure 65 a black-footed ferret is shown in drying position. Note how the front feet (claws) are held together with thread; insect pins are holding down the toes of the back feet and are inserted around the eyes to hold lids in place. A wire under the chin holds the animal upright until all has dried and set.

Fig. 64. Mounted squirrel entering nest.

Fig. 65. Mounted ferret; note pins holding eyes, thread wrapped around toes, wire holding mount upright until dry.

LARGE MAMMALS

Very few taxidermists today are called upon to mount large mammals—deer, moose, elk, antelope, bear, and so on. In olden days when a large animal was to be mounted, it was more than likely "stuffed." Most know the method that was used. Today, should the taxidermist be called upon to mount any large mammal, modeled forms of most can be purchased from taxidermy supply houses. For the "one-time" job this is the easiest, best, and cheapest method to use. Large-mammal taxidermy requires a knowledge of the habits of the animal being mounted and its anatomy, as well as experience in both modeling and casting. No one today—or if they do they shouldn't—mounts a large mammal by the "stuffing" method; if this method is employed the animal certainly looks "stuffed."

Skinning

Care in the skinning of the animal and care in taking measurements are *most important* in large-mammal taxidermy. In skinning, the opening incision/cuts are made from a point between the front legs to a point between the back legs; the skin is split open to the tip of the tail [Fig. 66 (A—B—C)]. The legs, both front and back, are cut open on the back, or underside, all the way to the hoof (D—E). In antlered animals the skin is cut open on top of the neck to the base of the horn, or antler, *never on the throat,* and the ears are skinned out (see Chapter 6, "Game Heads, Fur Rugs"). The skin is removed from the body in one piece.

Any blood or dirt is washed off with cold water before the

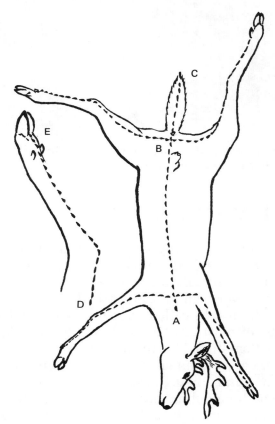

Fig. 66. Opening incisions, full mount (A—B—C); note incision back of each leg (D—E).

blood has a chance to set; this is *most important* with white goats, or any white/light-haired animal. The skin is now shaved as much as is possible in the field, all fat is removed, the ears turned, (see Chapter 6), the nostrils split open, and the skin worked down to the foot/hoof on each leg. Heavy flesh around the ear butts, the eyes, nostrils, and lips are cut away; the more work you can do now, the better the skin will be preserved until ready for tanning. The skin is now salted, making certain that the salt covers the entire flesh side of the skin. Roll up, flesh side in, and lay away in a cool place, never near the fire or in the sun. The next day, unroll, shake off excess salt, and resalt. Roll the skin up, and if in a humid climate this process may have to be done several times prior to shipping the skin to the tanner. Today, in all large-mammal taxidermy, the skins are tanned; in olden days these skins were just "pickled," which caused so many fine animal specimens, where the skins were "pickled" and the mammal "stuffed," to deteriorate—and the mounts became worthless. After the skin has been removed from the body, make as many measurements as you can, and if possible, plaster casts of the important anatomy, especially the face and leg muscles. These will be of help later if you are to model and cast and make the manikin to receive the tanned skin. If the entire skeleton of the animal can be roughed out in the field and shipped to the studio, this will simplify work—much of the guesswork in "setting" up the armature will be eliminated.

Mounting

Figure 67 shows the entire skeleton of a dog (greyhound), with all bones named. In the mounting of many big-game mammals (as illustrated later), the entire skeleton is used; this is a big help in getting the correct position and anatomy.

The method used today in all large-mammal taxidermy is one worked out by the well-known taxidermist, Carl Akeley, many years ago. This method of mounting is still referred to as the "Akeley" method. With knowledge of and experience in this method, you can mount a lifelike animal.

The *armature* is the foundation that will receive the clay used to model out the form and anatomy of the animal. Figure 68 shows the skeleton of a pronghorn (antelope). Note that the entire skeleton has been roughed out; all flesh and muscles have been cut away, the

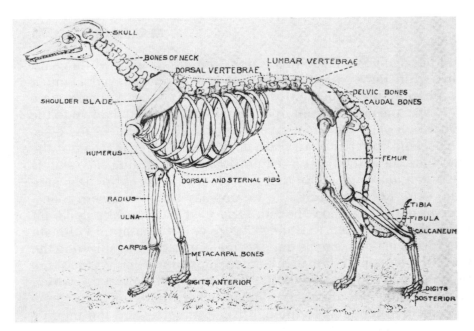

Fig. 67. Skeleton of a dog (greyhound); bones are indicated.

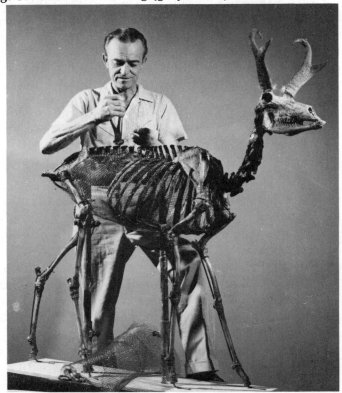

Fig. 68. Skeleton (pronghorn) set up for armature.

viscera removed, and the skeleton poisoned and given a coat of formaldehyde after being set up in the desired position in the finished mount. The skeleton, now called the armature, is held in position with iron rods anchored to a wood core fitted to the body cavity. The armature is the base/foundation over which the taxidermist now models the flesh/muscles of the body that were cut away when the animal was collected. The medium used is modeling clay.

Now the taxidermist's knowledge of the anatomy of the animal is called into play, as well as his experience in modeling. Working from photos, measurements, and knowledge of anatomy, the body of the animal is modeled in clay to the exact size, shape, and anatomy of the living animal. Note that with each position the animal is to take, the anatomy takes on a different muscular formation. This is the crucial stage—to turn out a well-mounted animal, the clay

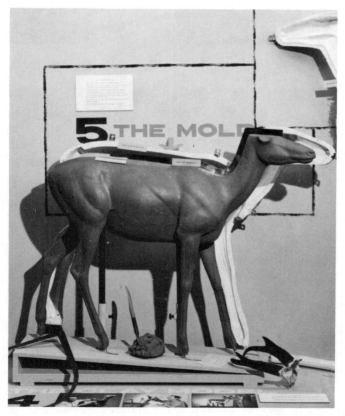

Fig. 69. Modeling clay (replaces flesh cut away) modeled over armature.

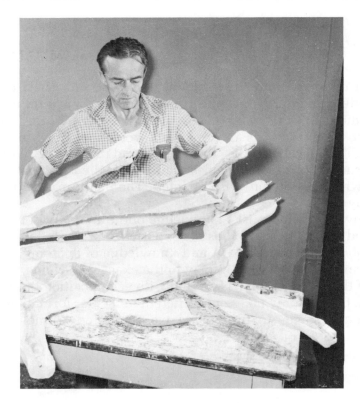

Fig. 70. Sectional plaster piece mold.

Fig. 71. Form to receive tanned skin; actual reproduction of animal's body after skin was removed.

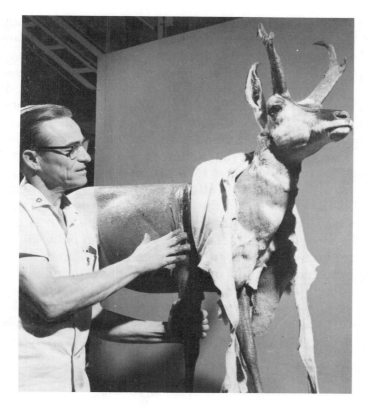

Fig. 72. Adjusting tanned skin over modeled form.

form must be as exact as was the body of the animal after the skin was removed. You can see now that it is much easier and more economical to purchase a body ready for the tanned skin. Figure 69 shows the modeled clay body of the pronghorn ready for casting the mold; you cannot put the skin over this clay form and expect it to hold up.

The plaster-of-Paris mold is made by first dividing the clay form into sections; thus, after the plaster has set, the mold can be pulled apart. This, the sectional mold, is made by first flowing plaster over each section of the model, then building up the sections with plaster dipped in coarse tow to add strength to the mold. After the plaster has set, the divided sections of the mold allow it to come apart (Fig. 70). The manikin is next made—it is this that will receive the tanned skin of the animal. In each section of the mold a layer of either heavy building paper or burlap is glued. This is followed by several layers of the paper or burlap, each layer put down with body paste (Formula #105) and built up thick enough to support the skin. Iron rods, threaded, of the proper size are now fastened in each of the sections for support and the sectional mold is put together. Seams are then plastered, and after all has set the mold is wet down with water until the manikin on the inside will come loose. Figure 71 shows the manikin of the pronghorn, an exact copy of the clay model, being given a coat of shellac to water-proof prior to pulling on and adjusting the tanned skin. The skin, after being received from the tanner, is relaxed and poisoned; the body paste (Formula #105) is then brushed over the manikin and the skin is pulled/adjusted until all is in its proper position. The paste holds the skin tight to the modeled anatomy of the manikin. Ear liners (see Chapter 6) are put in the ears, the skin is modeled around the face, and the incisions/cuts along the belly, on back of the neck, and down the legs are sewn together. In Figure 72 the skin is being adjusted over the manikin. The male pronghorn, along with two females, is shown in the completed habitat group (Fig. 73).

Figure 74 shows a white-tail deer (doe) mounted in 1904–05 by James L. Clark under the direction of Carl Akeley. This is one of

Fig. 73. Habitat group; pronghorn. [Milwaukee Public Museum photo.]

Fig. 74. White-tail deer (doe); mounted by James L. Clark in the early 1900s by the Akeley method of big-game mounts.

the first museum animals to be mounted by the Akeley method of big-game taxidermy. The photograph was taken recently, and one can see at once how the mount has remained in good condition over many years.

While this method has been touched on only briefly, it should be clear that mounting big game is not learned overnight. It takes years of experience and an intimate knowledge of the habits of animals. Complete instructions cannot be given in a book; success in large-mammal taxidermy will depend upon your willingness to invest years of practice in the art.

6 | GAME HEADS, FUR RUGS

The technique used in the mounting of heads of game animals as trophies for the sportsman and the making of fur rugs from their body skins are similar to those in mounting mammals. In the olden days of taxidermy, game heads were mounted by wrapping the natural skull of the animal with coarse excelsior, then covering it with clay, or a composition; the "pickled" scalp of the animal was then adjusted to this form. Even today, one can see examples of this technique—horrible examples, and in most cases specimens of an outstanding trophy head now worthless.

Today the modern taxidermist mounts game heads over a form—one modeled for that particular specimen or purchased from one of the many taxidermy supply houses. This is an easier and much cheaper method when one takes into consideration the time in labor and more important, the end result. When ordering forms, all measurements of the animal's head should be given, as well as the position you have in mind for the completed head mount. Head skins, or capes as they are sometimes referred to, must receive care in the skinning and preserving prior to being sent to the tanner. Today, all game head scalps/capes are tanned; it is very rare that a taxidermist will pickle a scalp if he/she wants to do a first-class job. After the animal has been collected, the skinning must not be delayed or the scalp will spoil before it can be tanned. If the hair starts to slip there are no known methods—secret or otherwise—that can save it.

SKINNING

The opening incision/cut is always made on the back of the neck on all game heads, *never on the throat*. Figure 75 shows the incision/cuts; from (A) to the base of each antler or horn, and from (B) to (C)

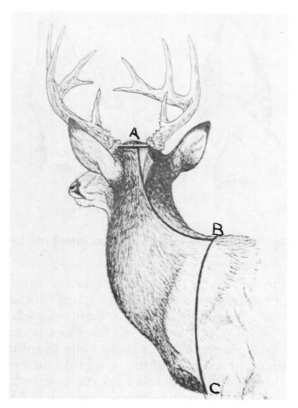

Fig. 75. Opening incision (A) base of each antler to (B) top of shoulder around brisket (C).

around the brisket. Leave the neck skin long, with most of the brisket attached. This makes a more attractive head mount. The scalp is removed from the head by first working the skin loose around the base of each antler with a blunt tool; then skin down to the ears and cut away each close to the skull. When the eyes, nostrils, and lips are reached *use extreme care*; the eyes are cut close to the skull and the nostrils and lips are cut away from the nose and jaws. Cut the lip linings close to the teeth and leave the nose cartlidge attached to the scalp. Remove the scalp (cape) all in one piece. Cut away all pieces of meat and fat left on the scalp and turn each ear inside out as one would remove a glove from the hand. This important step is shown in Figure 76: (A) shows where all meat has been cleaned from the ear butts and how the skin has been worked/cut from the base of each ear; (B) shows the ear turned inside out, skinned down to the tip, and the cartlidge removed,

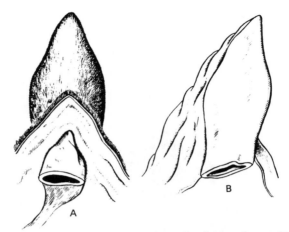

Fig. 76. Skinning ear (A); ear skinned out (B).

leaving only the ear linings. The ears can now be left turned inside out and the ear cartlidge can be used as a guide for the artificial ear linings to be made later or by making a tracing of each. The nostrils and lips must be split open so that salt used as a preservative prior to the tanning will penetrate. Use a sharp knife in splitting open the nostrils and lips and work carefully to avoid cutting through the skin. This is the most difficult and important part of the skinning operation, but one that must be done so the scalp will arrive at the tanners in good condition. By working slowly on your first attempt you will soon see that both nostrils and lips can be opened without many problems; if you do a good job, the tanner will surely return a good scalp.

After the scalp is cleaned of all meat and fat, turn the ears, split open the nostrils and lips, and rub salt over all parts on the flesh side. Now roll up the scalp, flesh side in, and leave over night. If the weather is damp, or the scalp is a large one, it is better to unroll the next day, shake off the excess salt, and resalt, again making certain the salt covers all the fleshy parts. Now you can roll it up and ship it off to the tanner. If you are careful in skinning and preparing the scalp prior to shipping to the tanner, you can expect a good tanning job.

As most all game heads today are mounted on ready-made forms, measurements must be taken of the head and neck after the scalp/cape has been removed. Measure the length from a point back of the antlers (or base of the skull) to the tip of the nose; from the corner of the eye to the tip of the nose; around the nose, back of the

Fig. 77. Antlers cut from skull; section of skull left attached.

nostrils, and under the jaws; around the neck at the base of the skull, and around the neck at the brisket. After the position of the mounted head is decided, all measurements that are taken will help in ordering the correct sized form.

The only part of the skull that is needed are the antlers, or horns. Figure 77 shows the cut made on top of the skull to remove the antlers. This cut, as shown, is made through the skull at the top of the eye sockets; this section of the skull is cleaned and used to hold the antlers when secured to the form. Glass eyes of the proper size and color must be ordered with the form; many of the taxidermy supply houses list the proper eyes for each game head. To insure getting the correct size, measure the eyes (in millimeters) when you skin the head.

MOUNTING

The "head-form" method is the easiest and most convenient (as well as labor-saving) way to mount all game heads. Figure 78 shows a head form for a white-tail deer; note that all anatomy of the face, around the eyes, nostrils, lips, and neck have been modeled in

Fig. 78. Modelled form (purchased from supply house) with antlers attached; eyes set in place.

the form. You can also see how the eyes are set in the eye sockets and held in place with composition (Formula #106). This composition will also allow you to model around the eyes to give the proper expression to the mounted head later. Take care in setting the eyes to their proper angle and depth, since the expression and lifelike appearance of any mount depends upon how the eyes are set in the form.

As you can see, purchasing these forms eases much of the work in the mounting of game heads.

Some of the forms come without a backboard, so this will now have to be cut and fitted. Trace the outline of the back of the neck onto a 1-inch piece of clear wood, saw out this area, and fit it into the neck opening of the form. Fasten by nailing through the form into the wood.

Fig. 79. Close-up; antlers attached to form.

The antlers are set in position on the form and held there by two 3-inch wood screws run through the skull section and into a block of wood cast in the form for this purpose. Figures 78 and 79 show the antlers in place on the form.

After the scalp has been returned by the tanner, it must be relaxed before it can be poisoned and pulled/adjusted over the form. Relax it by brushing on the flesh side the carbolic-acid-water solution (Formula #101), making certain all parts of the skin are well covered, especially the ears, nostrils, and lips. Roll up the skin and lay it away until it is soft and pliable and thoroughly relaxed. It will help to wrap the damp skin in plastic at this time. If the scalp has been well tanned, this relaxing will soon take place. If there are any cuts or tears in the skin they must first be sewn together using a small stitch that will not show. Be careful not to catch any of the hairs, as this will pull them out of position. When thoroughly relaxed the scalp must be poisoned (Formula #104). Even though the scalp has been tanned, it still must be poisoned. Brush on the solution over the flesh side, again making certain all parts of the scalp are well covered. It is now ready to be adjusted/pulled over the form.

Prior to pulling on the scalp, the form must be given a thin coat of body paste (Formula #105); this allows the scalp to be adjusted into position with ease and holds it secureley to the form. In Figure 80 the scalp is being pulled over and adjusted to the form. Note the antlers in place, the eyes set, and the form covered with the body paste. It is now up to the taxidermist to use his experience in getting all parts of the scalp to fit to their proper position on the form.

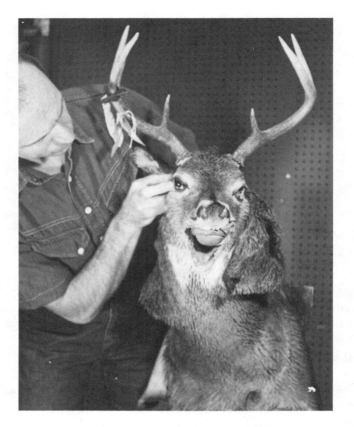

Fig. 80. Adjusting tanned skin over form.

In your first attempt at mounting a game head, you should work slowly and carefully. Try the relaxed and tanned scalp on the form before applying the body paste to be certain everything fits and to acquaint yourself with how the scalp will look after all is in place. Pull and stretch the skin, checking to make certain it drapes properly and that the hair pattern falls into place. Before the final fitting of the scalp to the form, artificial ear cartlidges must be fitted into the ears. These ear linings can be purchased when the form is ordered, or better yet can be cut from perforated lead. Using the tracings made from the original ear cartlidge, cut the artificial ear lining from lead and with body paste work each into the ears. Removing the cartlidge makes this job easy, and if the ear liners are of the correct size they will fit. Before fastening the ears to the form, use modeling composition (Formula #106) at the base of each ear butt; this is to insure that the ear butts can be modeled and will hold the artificial ears in position.

Figures 81 and 82 show the modeled form of a mule deer (with anatomy modeled on the form) and how the tanned scalp has been adjusted into position. Note in Figure 82 the eyes set in their correct position and the ears in place. As most of the modeling around the nostrils and lips has been put into the form, the skin of the mouth only has to be fitted in place. With some forms the opening/slit made to receive the skin of the lips will have to be enlarged; this should be done now so that the lip skin can be pushed into this opening and held there with small brads. The black markings of the lips should be the same on each side of the mouth.

The scalp can be held temporarily in place with twine and nails while adjusting into position; be sure that all air bubbles under the skin are worked out. Draw the scalp well up under the

Fig. 81. Sectional view (side) showing tanned skin on modelled form; antler, ear, eye in place.

Fig. 82. Sectional view (front) showing tanned skin on modelled form; antler, ear, eye in place.

antler burrs and hold it in place with nails until you are ready to sew the incision/cut on the back of the neck. Set the ears at the correct angle and insert a small wad of excelsior in the hollow of each ear to hold the skin in place until dry.

After the scalp is in place, the ears are in position, and the skin around the eyes, nostrils, and lips are modeled, the scalp can be sewn along the back of the neck. Using a furrier's curved needle and heavy waxed thread, sew the incision/cut together. Start at the base of the neck and work up to the point between the antlers, then to each cut at the base of the antler. Use small stitches in pulling the skin together. Allow enough of the neck skin at the brisket to turn back over the baseboard and tack the skin to the board, placing the nails close together.

Your attention should now be to giving the correct expression around the eyes. If the glass eyes have been set in the form at their correct angle and depth, this should be easy; all you will have to do is to hold the eye lids in place with small brads until dry. The nostrils and lips will have to be held to the form; but, again, since the modeling of both have been made in the form, you will only have to adjust them in place.

Wash off all body paste on the hair before it dries by sponging with warm water; clean any surplus paste around the eyes, nostrils, and lips. After the hair is clean and while still damp, brush it with a

Fig. 83. Complete mount; mule deer.

stiff hair brush to work the hair pattern in place. As the head dries, which may take several weeks depending upon the weather and head you are working with, give it your attention each day. If any extra modeling is needed around the eyes, nostrils, or lips, you should do this as the composition sets, not after. When thoroughly dry, remove all brads, cut off any loose ends of thread, and clean away all traces of composition, again with warm water. Use modeling wax (Formula #107) to model around the eyes, inside the nostrils and ears, and on any parts of the lips that may need to be built up; sometimes there is some shrinkage in drying. The wax will help model out these parts and render a more natural and lifelike appearance to the head. It is helpful to use a small modeling tool.

Comb and brush out the hair. To give the antlers a lifelike shine, oil them with the oil solution (Formula #108) with a soft cloth; now wipe off any surplus. Where the skin was waxed, or where there was color in the living animal, use oil colors to restore the natural look to the mounted head.

While some of these instructions may seem brief, it must be understood that as you progress you will see what needs to be done. Thus you may work out a better technique to fulfill your own needs and establish your own way of working. Again—the methods and/or techniques you use are not all-important; what *is important* is your ability and knowledge in mounting a game head to resemble the animal as it was in life. Figure 83 shows a game head of a mule deer mounted by the method just described.

FUR RUGS

Game animals, especially those of the bear and cat family, are often used as rugs; some are flat, others have open mouths. These skins, like scalps for head mounts, are also tanned (see Chapter 8). Figure 84 shows the opening incision/cuts made in a mammal skin for a rug. Start at a point under the lower jaw down the belly to the tip of the tail and from the center of the pad of each foot up and around the leg on the inside to the other foot; do the same for each leg. Remove the body skin in one flat piece; the same technique is used in skinning out the body, head, and feet as when the animal is to be mounted entire and/or for a game head. The importance in using care in skinning cannot be emphasized enough; save yourself extra work by not putting in cuts or tears in the skin. Remove all flesh and fat, salt the skin, and send it to the tanner. Skins for rugs, like

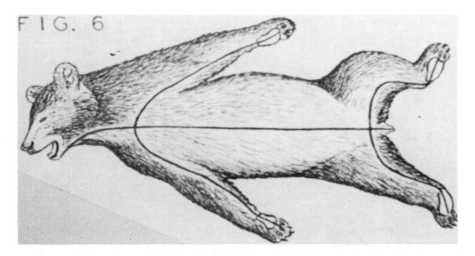

Fig. 84. Opening incision for rug and life-size mounts.

those used for mounting, must be tanned. As with game heads, you can save yourself much time and labor if you purchase a complete form for the head. A rug mounted with an open mouth will have a more dramatic effect. These head forms (for rugs) come with or without artificial teeth and tongue in place; also, most all come with the color of the inside of the mouth finished. These forms are made from a very light material, but are strong enough to withstand hard use while the rug is on the floor. Most come with modeling as in a finished game head form. The anatomy of the eyes, nostrils, and lips is worked out in the form.

Figure 85 shows the head form without teeth and tongue for a black bear, and Figure 86 shows the same form with artificial teeth and tongue in place. In Figure 87 the mounted head of the bear has a natural lifelike expression, which can be achieved with the use of these forms. Figure 88 shows the head form, with artificial teeth and tongue, of a tiger; the mounted head of the tiger using this form is pictured in Figure 89.

Some taxidermists will use the natural teeth of the animal in the mounting of heads for rugs; however, in time they will not only chip and crack but will turn yellow with age. It is much better to use artificial teeth; with today's technique of reproduction it is nearly impossible to tell the artificial teeth from the natural ones unless examined closely.

When the tanned skin has been returned from the tanner it must be relaxed with the carbolic-acid-water solution (Formula

Fig. 85. Head form, artificial teeth, and tongue for bear head, open mouth rug (from supply house).

#101), then poisoned with the preserving solution (Formula #104). Skins for rugs receive the same treatment as those for mounting, or for game-head mounts. After the skin has been relaxed, it is poisoned, allowing the solution to penetrate the skin. Another coat should be given to the head to make certain all parts are thoroughly covered. Prior to mounting, the head skin must be made pliable so it can be worked. Artificial ears can be cut from a piece of leather, not too thick or too thin (you should have made a tracing of the ear

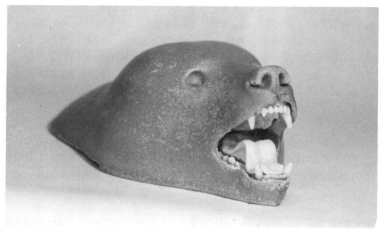

Fig. 86. Form with teeth and tongue in place.

Fig. 87. Mounted bear head, open mouth rug.

cartlidge removed from the ears when the animal was skinned); use the cartlidge as a guide for these leather linings. First insert the ear linings in each ear. Use leather, or some similar material, so that when the rug is on the floor it will not break if stepped upon. Cover the head form, with the artificial teeth and tongue in place, with a thin coat of body paste (Formula #105); then pull the skin and

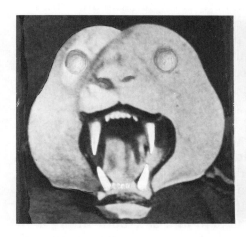

Fig. 88. Head form tiger; artificial teeth and tongue in place (from supply house).

Fig. 89. Mounted tiger head; open mouth for rug.

adjust it in position. Using the paste will make it easier to adjust the skin to the form and will hold everything in position until dry.

Now you can work the modeling composition (Formula #106) under the skin around the eyes, nostrils, and lips to model the expression of the face; use small brads to hold the skin in place on the form. Set proper colored glass eyes into the eye sockets in the form and carefully give the correct angle and depth; this is important in giving the face a natural look (Figs. 87 and 89). Comb and brush out the hair and allow to dry before finishing the body skin into a rug.

After the mounted head is thoroughly dry, the body skin must be relaxed again by brushing on the flesh side the *carbolic-acid-water* solution. Brush plenty of this solution on the skin, but do not let it run off onto the hair side. Roll up, flesh side in, and allow to remain over night, longer for a larger skin; repeat the process if necessary—the skin must be made pliable for working. Now stretch the skin on a table larger than the skin, or on the floor, and pull and stretch the skin flat, holding everything in place with nails around the edges. Place the nails close together so that the skin is stretched evenly and without wrinkles. In most cases it will be necessary to make a series of V-cuts in the skin where the wrinkles occur. In Figure 90 (*A*) these V-shaped pieces of skin are cut away; the edges will later be sewn together. If properly done, the wrinkles will work out and the skin will lie flat. It may be necessary to make another V-cut at the base of the head (*B*), so the head will lie in a straight line. After the skin has been stretched full and flat, and all wrinkles have been cut out and these cuts sewn together, allow to dry in this position. *Do not remove the nails until the skin is thoroughly dry.*

After the skin has dried, remove all nails, turn the skin over, and poison again on the flesh side. There are several ways to finish off a rug, although today most rugs are finished without the "fancy" felt border used some years ago. A good grade of cotton padding should be placed underneath the body skin to "pad out" the skin and to prevent wear. Trim the padding to the outline of the rug, with an extra layer of padding under each foot, and sew it securely to the body skin. It is not necessary to sew the padding completely around the edges, only enough to hold so the skin will not come loose, or the padding bunch up. If you want a felt border, select a color that will harmonize with the skin and sew both lining and border to the body skin at the same time. Use a strong, waxed thread and a furrier's curved needle and make the stitches close together so the skin will not gap open. Figure 91 shows the body

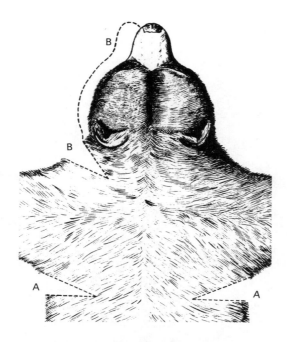

Fig. 90. Cuts in tanned skin (A) to remove wrinkles; in skin (B) so head will lie straight.

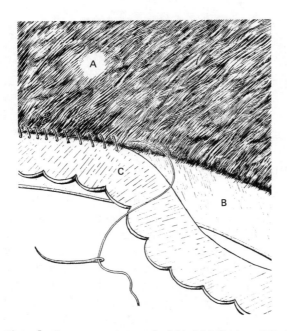

Fig. 91. Sectional view, rug: tanned skin (A) lining (B); felt border (C).

93

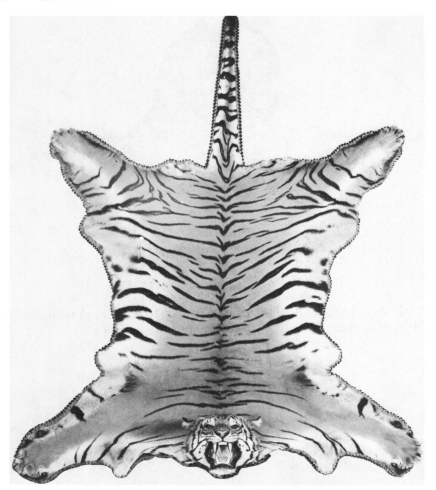

Fig. 92. Complete rug, open-mouth Bengal tiger.

skin (A), the lining (B), and the felt border (C) all being sewn at the same time.

Now turn the rug over and comb and brush the hair until all falls into place; brush out any dust. To restore the colors of the eyes, lips, and nostrils use oil colors of the proper shade. Your fur rug (unless displayed hanging on the wall) will be subject to much wear; comb and brush regularly to keep it in good condition. You should also take it out to air whenever possible. Figure 92 shows an excellent example of a tiger rug. (This animal is now protected all over the world.) Here the use of a felt border enhances the appearance of the finished rug.

7 | FISH, REPTILES

Another branch of taxidermy becoming popular and profitable today for the taxidermist is the mounting of fish. Many different species of fish are being caught by the sportsman; some catches are outstanding specimens, and they should be mounted. Fish taxidermy has progressed through the years by different techniques—mounts using the skin; mounts where the specimen is cast, then reproduced in various materials (this method is very seldom used in mounts for fishermen, but such mounts are found in museums), and another method whereby the specimen is cast and this cast used as a study/model to carve the body of different materials such as balsa wood or styrafoam. There is also another method, quite recently developed, whereby the fish is cast and a reproduction made in fiberglass.

The following method is one that can be used by both amateur and professional; if the directions are carefully followed you can end up with a fairly good mount. But as in all other branches of taxidermy, it is your knowledge in the finishing/coloring of a mount that will help you turn out an exceptional job. To be good in fish taxidermy, study the coloring of the live specimen when it is taken from the water; making your color notes rapidly before these colors change. Most all colors in fish fade soon after it is removed from its natural environment.

COLOR NOTES

Record the colors of the fish (again, as soon as possible) with colored crayons, water or oil colors, and/or written notes. If only written notes are used, you must be familiar with colors by name and able to record them correctly. One of the best methods is to make an outline of the fish; then color it in with either crayons or paints, or record the colors with written notes. At this time *be sure* to record the eye colors.

CASTING

Keep the specimen in a cool place—better still, well iced. If placed in an ice chest, first wrap in a damp cloth, wet moss, or grass and keep in this condition until ready for work. *Do not* gut any fish (unless the larger game fish such as sailfish, marlin, tarpon, etc.) prior to casting. The fish should be cast and skinned as soon as is possible—colors fade and the body will shrink quickly. For your first attempt select one of the hard-scale, nonfat specimens, such as a large- or small-mouth bass or perch.

Prior to making the cast, the show side of the fish must be chosen; this is, of course, the best side. If there have been any shrunken contours in the belly, slit open on the *off side* and fill out to the proper roundness with sand, wet moss, or grass. The specimen must be in perfect condition before casting. Have a box or pan of fine sand (larger than the fish you are about to cast) in which to lay out the fish, but first wash off the slimy mucus (that all fish are covered with) in clear, running water using a soft cloth; work from the head down toward the tail. Do this several times; wash out the mouth and gills thoroughly. The specimen must be clean and all mucus removed. As a final rinse use a saturate solution of salt water over the entire specimen.

Lay a newspaper on the sand, and upon this lay the fish *show side up* and posed in the position you want the mount to be displayed; you can build up the body with sand underneath. If the mouth is to be shown open, fill the cavity with sand to keep out the plaster. At this time remove the pectoral fin [Fig. 93 (*A*)] and keep it wet. Spread all the fins and the tail, holding them in position with long pins or wires. *Remember:* the position of the mount cannot be changed once you have started the cast/mold.

Mix enough plaster-of-Paris to cover the fish. This mixing of the plaster is most important, either in making a fish cast/mold or a plaster mold for other purposes. Always use the same technique in mixing plaster so it will not only be well mixed but if used for reproductions, it will hold all detail of the specimen being cast. Put enough cold water in a large bowl for the job you are now taking on. Sift, *do not pour in,* plaster until a cone of the plaster rises above the surface of the water line. Allow the water to absorb the plaster

Fig. 93. Specimen positioned, show side; pectoral fin removed (*A*).

Fig. 94. Plaster being poured for body mold.

Fig. 95. Plaster mold; allow to set.

before you start to mix, then mix only by "cutting" back and forth with a spoon or knife. Do not mix by bringing up batches of plaster above the water line, as this will tend to mix in air bubbles. This "kills" the mix, making what is known as a soft mold.

Shortly after the plaster is sifted into the water, a chemical action begins to harden the plaster. This process causes the mixture to heat up; the hardness of the cast/mold can be judged by this heating of the plaster. The plaster should be of the consistency of thick cream; experience will tell you just how much plaster to mix for each job. All plaster should be mixed at the same time. Now, starting at the head of the fish, pour or spoon on the plaster, working toward the tail, but do not entirely cover the fins, or, tail. Make the cast/mold heavy enough that it will not break when removed from the fish (Fig. 94). In Figure 95 the plaster mold is covering the fish. Allow the plaster to set (this happens when the mold feels warm to the touch, but remove before the mold gets hot), and remove the fish specimen. Do not leave it in the mold any longer than necessary.

SKINNING THE FISH

Turn the mold over and remove the fish by picking it up by the tail. Carefully work it from the mold so that the scales will not become damaged. Lay the mold aside for later use (Fig. 96). Wash off all plaster from the fish and lay it out on a clean piece of paper or a clean table. Figure 97 shows the opening incision/cut being made on the *off side* from the back of the head between the supracleithrum and cleithrum bones (A) to the base of the tail (B). Make the cut only through the skin, not into the flesh. Carefully remove the skin by first working it down over the back, then over the belly, using the scalpel and/or the bone cutters around the fins and tail. Keep the skin flat at all times while skinning. Do not leave any meat on the skin and keep the skin, especially the fins and tail, wet at all times when skinning (Fig. 98). Detach the tail from the body [Fig. 99 (A)] and skin down over the back until the head is reached (B). The body can now be discarded (unless you want it for food); in this method only the skin is used, the mount/shape of the fish being guided by the cast/mold.

All particles of flesh remaining on the skin must be scrapped off using a dull knife or a skin scrapper. Cut away all flesh from base of the fins and tail and trim close to the skin. In scrapping the skin be careful not to injure the silvery lining found on the inside of the skin—this is important to the outside coloring. Work from the tail toward the head to keep the scales in their sockets. Cut away all flesh from around base of the skull; cut out the brain cavity, but leave the skull intact. *Do not* remove the gills (Fig. 100). Turn the

Fig. 96. Specimen being removed from body mold.

Fig. 97. Opening incision $(A-B)$ on off side.

Fig. 98. Skinning specimen.

100

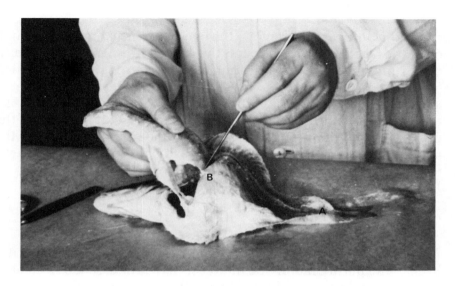

Fig. 99. Skinning, tail detached (*A*); skin down to head (*B*).

Fig. 100. Cleaning inside of skin.

101

cleaned skin over and remove the eyes and cheek muscles, which can now be cleaned out through the eye cavities. Wash the skin in cold, running water; if greasy, immerse it in the degreasing solution (Formula #103) for about one-half hour (depending on size of specimen), then drain and "dip" it in alcohol, which tends to "set" the skin. The skin is next preserved by immersing it in either of the preserving solutions (Formula #104). At the base of the tail, on the fins, and around the head and gills brush on a coat of full-strength formaldehyde.

MOUNTING

After the skin has been cleaned, degreased, and poisoned, place it back in the plaster mold. The mold acts as a guide, so the skin takes on the natural contour of the live fish that was cast. If the mold has dried out, soak it in water; this will help to keep the fish skin relaxed while working. Hold the fins and tail in their proper positions with long pins or wires (Fig. 101). Mix a quantity of papier-mâché (which may be purchased from taxidermy supply houses) or use the modeling composition (Formula #106). Now flow or model a layer over the inside of the skin. Cut a small block of soft wood (which will be used later to hold fish to the panel) and press it into

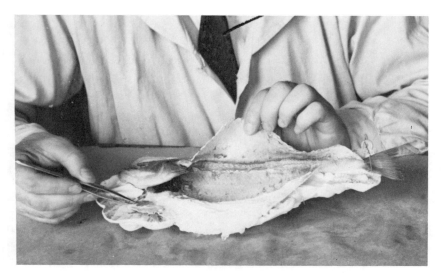

Fig. 101. Adjusting cleaned and poisoned skin into body mold.

the mâché/composition while it is still soft [Fig. 102 (A)]. Continue to fill the skin with the mâché/composition until the skin is nearly full in and around the wood block, and work it into the base of the skull. Do not overfill, but let the mold act as a guide at this point (Fig. 102).

Next, sew up the incision and shape the specimen. Start from the tail and sew toward the head. Keep the fins and tail wet and relaxed. Fill in the cheek muscles on the off side (the one you are now working on) with the mâché/composition through the eye cavity. Work fast while the mâché/composition is still soft, but if delayed keep the fish damp and relaxed. While the fish is still in the mold, model the mâché/composition through the skin; the mold will act as a guide in the final shaping of the fish specimen (Fig. 103).

As soon as the mâché/composition has set, remove the fish from the mold (Fig. 104). Now fill in the cheek muscles on the show side, filling through the eye cavity, and sponge off the specimen with alum water until clean (Formula #109). The fins and tail should have been kept relaxed while the above steps were taken; now pin them out and card them. Fasten the specimen to a temporary board, larger than the fish, using wood screws through the board into the

Fig. 102. Wood block for support (A); composition to fill skin.

Fig. 103. Incision sewn; specimen in mold for shape.

wood core that was set into the fish skin. Give to the fins and tail the angle wanted, but do not spread either into an unnatural spread, which is a common fault in fish taxidermy. Hold in position with pins or wires after fins/tail have been set between two pieces of waxed cardboard. Keep it in this position until dry. The pectoral fin that was removed prior to making the cast/mold can now be pinned out also between the cardboards and fastened to the fish in its

Fig. 104. Removing specimen after composition has set.

proper position; hold the pectoral fin with small pointed wires. The mouth can be opened—again, do not spread the mouth open too much. (In many mounted fish the mouth has been opened wide, giving the specimen an unnatural look.) Spread the gills, and hold both the mouth and gills in the desired position with small blocks of wood or pieces of styrafoam. At this time make certain that the fish, fins, tail, and mouth are in the position wanted: when the mâche/composition sets, no changes can be made. Now set it away to dry, which may take several weeks depending upon the specimen and the weather.

The fish must be thoroughly dry before finishing and coloring. After this step, the fins and tail should be made strong and flexible. Use a mixture of carpenter's glue and glycerine (one-fourth glue to the amount of water) to keep the glue flexible and a light-grade cloth and jeweler's tissue (or a similar grade) for backing on the fins and tail. Glue a strip of the cloth to the underside of all fins and tail, and glue the tissue to the top side of each. It is best to tear, instead of cut, both the cloth and tissue so that a ragged edge will be on the top side of fins and tail; this will help in blending in the cloth and tissue when coloring so a line will not show. Make certain while gluing that all air bubbles are worked out from under both the cloth and tissue (Fig. 105). After the glue has set, the specimen can be removed from the board and placed upon a screened box (frame) so that the fish can dry out thoroughly, top and bottom. Before

Fig. 105. Tail and fins strengthened with paper and cloth.

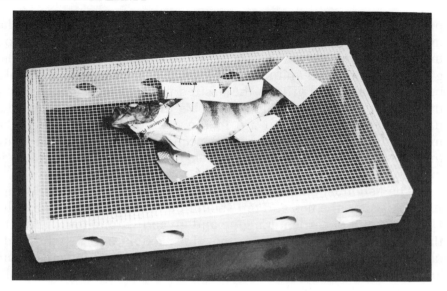

Fig. 106. Specimen on tray to dry.

coloring/painting make sure it is dry and all dirt and dust are removed (Fig. 106).

DIFFERENT METHOD

In another method of fish mounting in use by some taxidermists, the cast fish mold is used as a pattern/form and the artificial body is

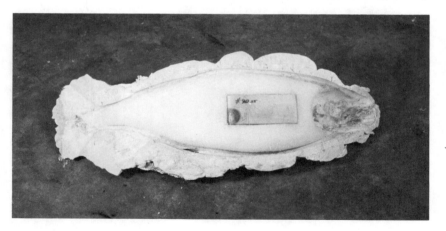

Fig. 107. Another method; body carved from styrofoam, wood block for support.

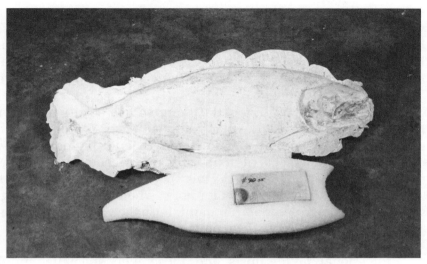

Fig. 108. Artificial body; mold acts as pattern.

cut/shaped from styrafoam. A small block of wood is inserted in the styrafoam and held in place with glue to hold the specimen to the panel later. These steps are illustrated in Figures 107 and 108. The skin, after it is cleaned, degreased, and poisoned, is then stretched over this styrafoam form, adjusted into position, and sewn. Then the fins and tail are carded and pinned out as previously described and placed to dry upon the screened box; when it is dry it can be colored/painted.

FINISHING THE SPECIMEN

After the fish has dried thoroughly, when the fins and tail have set, and once the glue holding the cardboard and tissue dry, you can trim off the surplus cloth and tissue. In trimming/outlining the fins and tail, use a sharp pair of scissors; the trimming is most important. *Do not cut in a straight line*, but follow the natural outline of the fins and tail. If you do not do this the finished mount will look unnatural. No matter how careful you work, you will find areas around the fins, tail, and head that will need modeling; also some scales will have to be replaced (modeled in) with modeling wax (Formula #107). Fill out all shrunken areas with the wax and model in any scales that are missing. Now insert proper colored glass eyes in the eye cavities (if only one side of the fish is to show, then only the eye on the show side is replaced)—again using the wax to hold them in place and to model around the eye. Build up the cheek muscles if needed and model in the mouth and around the gills. Be sure the fish looks as if it was just taken from the water before you restore the natural colors. Now give the specimen a very light coat of white shellac.

In the coloring/painting of the mounted fish no amount of written instructions can take the place of experience. You may turn out a natural-looking mount and then fail in coloring/painting—so, again, as with all aspects of taxidermy, experience, trial and error, and *practice* are what count. At this stage, you can at once see the advantage of taking accurate color notes when the fish was caught. Refer to these color notes as you paint. I use the word "paint," but it should be "tint,"—more fish (and good mounts) are ruined by "painting."

Professional taxidermists and those who specialize in fish mounts use an air brush in coloring. I think this method gives lifelike coloring to the mount. Most taxidermists, however, do not have, nor can they use, an air brush; they must resort to hand coloring/painting/tinting with oil colors thinned with linseed oil, turpentine, or a preparation known as "Megilp" (from artists' supply stores). Some taxidermists achieve good results using water colors and colored pencils, but this takes additional experience. Do not try to color the fish—that is, to color on all the colors at the same

Fig. 109. Mounted bluegill.

Fig. 110. Mounted yellow perch; mouth opened too wide.

time. With some species the base colors need to dry before the top, or pattern colors, can be applied. After all colors have been put on according to your color notes, allow the specimen to dry thoroughly; then give it several coats of a clear varnish, *thinned,* or one of several brands of clear plastic from an aerosol can. Spray on several coats; spray very lightly and allow to dry between coats.

The mount is now finished, and can be placed upon a suitable panel, or hung directly on the wall. As the end result you should

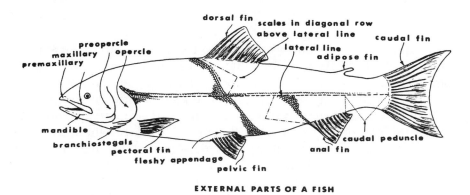

EXTERNAL PARTS OF A FISH

Fig. 111. Parts of fish identified.

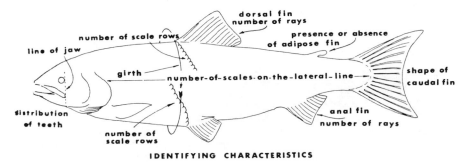

IDENTIFYING CHARACTERISTICS

Fig. 112. Characteristics of fish.

have a good mount and one fairly correct in coloring as your first attempt at fish taxidermy. Figure 109 shows a well-mounted and colored bluegill; Figure 110, a mounted yellow perch (but note the unnatural position of the mouth, which has been opened too wide—a common fault with some mounted fish). Figure 111 shows the external parts of a fish and Figure 112 the identifying characteristics.

LARGE GAME FISH

Few taxidermists, unless specializing in fish taxidermy, are ever faced with the task of mounting large game fish—the saltwater variety such as sailfish, tarpon, and marlin. Mounting such fish requires a different technique than that used in smaller specimens, due not only to size and weight but also the texture of the skin. In mounting a sailfish, the "sail," or dorsal fin, must be taken into consideration.

First choose the show side of the fish; then "sail" (if a sailfish) and the pectoral and ventral fins are carefully removed from the body and kept relaxed/pliable in the carbolic-acid-water solution (Formula #101). Lay the fish out on its show side on the sand, or any flat surface larger than the specimen (if a board or cement, a separator of oil or grease will first have to be brushed on so the plaster mold will not adhere to this surface). Give the fish the natural appearance/shape you want in the completed mount. If there have been changes in body anatomy, such as shrinkage and wrinkles, open the fish on its *off side* and fill out the belly and other areas with sand.

Now clean the fish of all dirt with water and remove the mucus with the alum-water solution (Formula #109). Flow a heavy mixture of plaster-of-Paris over the entire body of the fish to form a strong, thick mold. The mold should extend from just beyond the eye to a point where the tail joins the body. The plaster mold is now reinforced with 1-inch by 1-inch strips of wood (or if a large fish, lengths of pipe) running lengthwise along the outside of the mold; the mold can now be handled without breaking [Fig. 113 (B)].

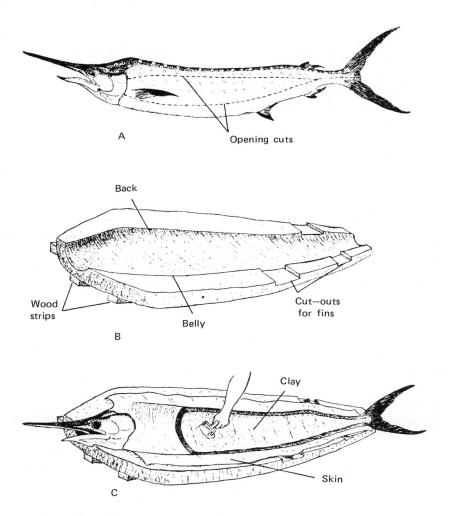

Fig. 113. Opening incision (A) on off side. Plaster mold (B) made prior to skinning on show side. Skin cleaned and poisoned in mold; clay being worked onto skin (C).

Allow the plaster to set thoroughly, then carefully turn it over and remove the fish from the mold.

Make the opening incision/cut on the *off side* [Fig. 113 (A)] and remove the skin as you would with smaller fish. The skin should now be cleaned of all flesh, the eyes and gills removed, and the flesh particles and muscles around the head and base of the fins and tail cut away. It is *most important* that all flesh be cleaned from the skin. Next wash the skin in cold, running water, drain, and salt dry. The use of salt toughens the skin, and it must be rubbed all over the flesh side after the skin has been cleaned.

Turning now to the mold, if any bubbles appear on the inside they must be filled in with plaster. When dry, smoothe the mold with coarse sandpaper. Cut sections from the mold for fins to fit when the skin is put back in the mold [Fig. 113 (B)]. Allow the skin to dry for several days (depending upon its size and weather); then wash off all salt thoroughly. Next, carefully fit the skin, while still damp and relaxed, into the plaster mold, making certain that all parts of the skin fit to the mold. Now poison with the preserving solution (Formula #104). Using a soft water clay (modeling clay made pliable with water added), push the clay all over the inside of the skin with your hands; this keeps the skin tight against the inside of the plaster mold and in position [Fig. 113 (C)]. Do not apply the clay too thick; about 1 inch is sufficient for a sailfish. While working keep the fins and tail wet and relaxed.

Again mix a batch of plaster-of-Paris and pour it over the clay in the mold, forming a core which will hold both clay and skin tight against the inside of the mold. The plaster core will be removed later. Do not use more plaster than is necessary to do the job. After the plaster has set, place a board, larger than the fish, over the back of the mold and carefully turn everything over. The board will support the skin, clay, and core, preventing anything from falling out. Now remove the plaster mold; the fins and tail left attached to the skin are now stretched into position and fastened to the board between heavy waxed cardboard and held in place with sharpened wires.

Allow the fish to dry; this will take several days or weeks. After completely dry, place the plaster mold back over the fish in its original position. Turn everything over and first remove the plaster core, then the clay, from inside the skin. Allow the fish to dry in this state for several more days, checking to see that the skin does not pull away from inside the mold. If this should happen, dampen the skin with carbolic-acid-water solution and hold that part against the mold with clay and plaster until set. Now brush out all dirt and dust from inside the skin, making certain it is clean. With papier-mâché or modeling composition (Formula #106) cover the inside of the skin with a thin coat and allow to dry. Brush in several layers of this mâché/composition, allowing each coat to dry before adding another. Shape a block of hardwood to conform to the inside of the mold and set it in place with more of the mâché/composition. The wood core serves as a base to support the specimen later.

Now sew the skin together and allow to dry; drying may take days or weeks. The fins that have been removed prior to making the cast should have been kept relaxed, and now will have to be shaped and dried into position. The "sail" is spread; after it is dry it is glued to a piece of $\frac{1}{8}$-inch plywood with carpenters glue (add 10% glycerine to the glue to keep it flexible and to prevent cracking). Hold the "sail" in position with thin strips of wood and wires/nails until dry, then cut along the natural outline of the "sail" and bevel the edges of the plywood. Mounting the "sail" on a wood base not only holds it in position but insures a good, strong support. When the specimen has dried thoroughly, make a cut the length of the "sail" along the back of the mounted fish where the "sail" was on the fish and set it into place. Hold it there with wood screws through the plywood and into the wood core.

Set glass eyes in the eye sockets and hold there with modeling wax; the wax can be used also to model around the eye and to fill in any shrinkage around the face, fins, and the base of the tail. After all modeling has been done, smooth with fine sandpaper dipped in

Fig. 114. Atlantic sailfish.

benzene to remove scratches made by the sandpaper. Color the fish with oil paints, following the color notes you made when the fish was removed from the water. The base color and any pattern the fish had in life is also painted/tinted on to give to it a lifelike appearance. Figure 114 shows a sailfish mounted by the method given.

FIBERGLASS FISH

One of the newest products, if not the newest in the reproduction of fish specimens, is fiberglass. Like many new techniques in taxidermy and other professions, it has its place; good for some mounts, but not for others, especially the mounting of fish for the fisherman. Many fish specimens do not turn out as they should as skin mounts, such as the saltwater and other oily specimens; these are most impossible to degrease. Here the fiberglass method is helpful, although you will have to convince the fisherman to accept a reproduction instead of the real thing.

As this method is not true taxidermy and, as it is somewhat technical, listed below are helpful publications.

> "Fiberglass vs. Skin Mounts" by Archie Phillips (order from: Archie Phillips, 200 52nd Street, Fairfield, AL 35064)
> "Fiberglass Fish" by Archie Phillips (order from: Archie Phillips, 200 52nd Street, Fairfield, AL 35064)
> "Fun with Fish" by Bob Frankowiak (order from: Milwaukee Public Museum, 800 West Wells Street, Milwaukee, WI 53223)
> "Fiberglas Fish Reproductions" by Clint Scott: (order from American Taxidermist Magazine, P.O. Box 11186, Albuquerque, N.M. 87112)

SNAKES

Many excellent mounts of snakes seen in some museums today are reproductions in plastics. This is a most complicated process, although it is the only one that can give a lifelike translucent color to the specimen; but it would be impossible to give this technique in written instructions. Today, only the Field Museum of Natural History (Chicago) has successfully used this technique, and no taxidermist there at this writing can duplicate the so-called "Walters" technique, named after the man who first worked out this method for the reproduction of reptiles, fish, and the fleshy parts of mammals.*

For all practical purposes, if the taxidermist is called upon to mount a snake, much the same technique can be used as in fish mounting. Care in the selection of the base—rock, log, sand—and in the pose of the snake should be exercised. Do not pose the snake in an extreme position, or you will find it difficult to remove later from the plaster mold. And, as with fish, make accurate notes of both color and pattern when the specimen is collected.

After the base is chosen, cover it with a piece of wax paper and place the snake on it in a natural pose, fitting the coils carefully to the contour of the wax-paper-covered base. Mix a batch of plaster-of-Paris and flow over the specimen following the same technique used in the casting/molding of a fish specimen. When the plaster has set, carefully remove the snake from the mold. Now remove the skin by an incision/cut down the belly from the center of the lower jaw to the tip of the tail. In this operation use care in removing the skin from the body. Clean off any flesh particles, wash in cold, running water, and preserve as with fish. The skin can also be immersed for a short time in the preserving solution (Formula #102), into which one should add approximately 5 parts powdered borax. Now fit the skin back into the mold; the mold again acts only as a "form" to hold the snake skin in its natural pose. Fill the skin very carefully with papier-mâché or the composition.

Instead of the block of wood you used in mounting the fish, bend two or three wires (length of snake to determine how many wires needed) in a U shape and set them in at different places along the belly with the ends of the wires protruding through the skin where the incision is to be sewn together. You will use these wires for anchoring the snake to the base later. Now begin at the tail and sew the incision/cut together using a very fine stitch.

Brush off any dirt/dust and allow the specimen to dry; this will take several days/weeks, depending upon the specimen and the weather. Colors can be restored with oil or water colors by referring to your notes. Again, as in fish mounting, use care in the painting/coloring to avoid giving the mount a painted look.

---

* This process has been described in detail in the pamphlet "New Uses of Celluloid and Similar Material in Taxidermy," by Leon L. Walters. Published as Museum Technique Series, No. 2, by the Field Museum of Natural History (Chicago), June 1925.

ANOTHER METHOD

If desired, a reproduction of the snake skin can be made in either plaster or wax. This is an easy technique and often employed by taxidermists. Many times this reproduction is so lifelike that the specimen must be examined closely to tell that it is a reproduction.

After you have posed the snake and made the plaster mold, the skin is no longer needed. If you use this method you must make a more careful plaster mold; all detail and anatomy of the snake must now be preserved in the plaster mold. When the mold is thoroughly dry, coat the inside with a separator—petroleum jelly (thinned) or liquid soap—and make certain that all parts of the mold are covered. If you are making a wax cast the separator will not be used—it is used only when casting in plaster. Now mix a small amount of plaster and flow into the mold. Do not fill the mold; use just enough plaster to cover the mold in a thin layer. Immediately rock the mold back and forth so the plaster covers the inside of the cast entirely in a thin layer. When the plaster has partly set, flow in more plaster (a different mix) and build up the mold to the size of the snake specimen. Set in the U-shaped wires and allow all to set. If making a wax cast, warm the dry mold, melt casting wax (from taxidermy supply houses), and flow this melted wax in the warm mold all at one time. Set in the wires and allow the wax to cool and harden. In making a plaster or wax reproduction, after both have set hard, immerse everything—mold with the reproduction on the inside—in water and leave it until the plaster absorbs as much of the water as it will. Now you can break the plaster mold away from the reproduction, but you must do this part of the work very carefully. Apply colors as previously described.

FROGS

Very few taxidermists are ever called upon to mount a frog. Should the situation arise, the best method is to make a reproduction, especially if it is a small frog such as a tree or green-frog. The reproduction is made by the same technique as the casting and reproduction of snakes (previously described). Mounting a large bullfrog can be done by skinning and mounting. In Figure 115 the opening incision/cut is shown as the dotted line (A-B); the body is skinned out through this opening, leaving the skull attached to the skin. When you reach the legs, cut them off from the body at (C), then

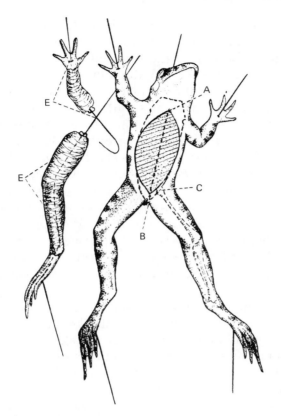

Fig. 115. Opening incision (A—B); leg bone cleaned of flesh, wrapped with tow, and anchored to wood core (C); leg bones wrapped with tow (E).

skin down to the feet but leave the feet attached to the skin. Clean off all flesh and muscles from the leg bones down to the feet. Now turn your attention to the skull and cut away all flesh, cut out the tongue, and remove the eyes through the eye cavities. Leave the skin attached to the top of the skull. At this time all flesh must be removed from the skin.

Wash the skin in cold, running water to remove all blood and body juices, then dip in alcohol—this tends to "set" the skin. Now immerse the skin in the preserving solution, or use solution (Formula #102) with borax added. Work this solution in with the hands so the skin will be well covered. Remove and allow to drain, but not dry; keep the skin relaxed at all times with the carbolic-acid-water solution (Formula #101). The skin of the frog must be kept damp and relaxed at all times while working.

In mounting, select five wires of the proper size for support and sharpen each on one end. Turn each leg inside out and run the wires through the bottom of the feet and along the bones; tie wire and bones together and wrap with fine tow to replace the flesh/muscles that have been cut away. Now cover all with a coat of soft modeling composition (Formula #106). Place a small amount of the composition at the base of the feet and turn the legs back into the leg skins. Figure 115 (E) shows the front and back legs wired and the tow/composition modeled onto the leg bones. From a small piece of balsa wood or other soft wood, carve/shape a body similar in size and anatomy to the original. Use the last wire and run it through this balsa body core and anchor it in place; then fit this core into the skin and run the wire up into and through the skull and anchor all leg bones in place (Fig. 115). Use composition to fill out where the skull and legs are anchored to the artificial body and to fill in any cavities showing; now sew up the incision/cut with small stitches.

Now shape the frog into position. Set glass eyes of the proper color and size in the eye sockets and hold them there with composition. Allow the specimen to dry. While the skin is still relaxed it is advisable to perforate the skin thoroughly in several places with a needle so it will dry slowly from inside out. After the specimen is dry, use modeling wax (Formula #107) to cover the incision and to build up/model any depressions or shrinkage that have occurred

Fig. 116. Bullfrog.

while drying. Now give the frog a coat of white shellac; and working from your color notes, apply the proper colors to give to the specimen the lifelike colors as it had in life (Fig. 116).

TURTLES

Your first attempt at mounting a turtle should prove satisfactory, since the shell constitutes most of the specimen. However, the shell limits the number of positions in which the turtle can be posed, but

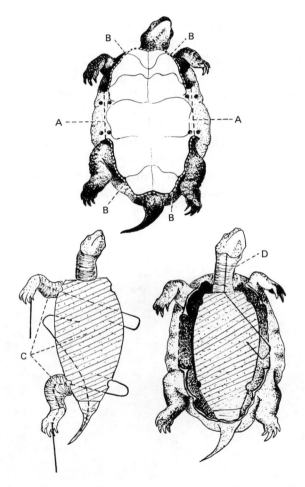

Fig. 117. Incision, bottom plate (A—A); incision, skin (B—B). Wood body core, legs anchored (C). Wood core, head and neck anchored (D).

then a turtle cannot and does not take on too many different positions.

In skinning, only the bottom plate, called the "plastron," is removed; the legs, tail, and head remain attached to the upper shell, called the "carapace." In Figure 117, lines (A-B) show where the plate is attached to the shell. Separate along this line by sawing at (A) and cut the skin loose around the upper and lower edges of the plate at (B); remove the plate from the body. Before sawing and cutting away the plate, drill four holes in both plate and shell (Fig. 117). These holes will later be needed when wiring the plate in place to the mounted turtle. After removing the plate, skin out the legs and tail by turning back the skin as you work. Flesh and muscles of the legs and tail are now cut away, as are the leg bones. Skin out the tail to the tip and remove the bone. Skin out the neck until the skull is reached; remove the skull cutting away the neck muscles at the base of the skull. You cannot skin over a turtles head, so the eyes, brain, tongue, and face muscles must be removed from in back of the skull and through the mouth. Wash the skin, shell, and plate in cold, running water until cleaned of all blood and body juices; then dip them in alcohol, drain, and immerse in the preserving solutions. Keep all parts wet and relaxed while working.

Cut four wires of proper size and length to support the mount and sharpen each on one end; these will be the leg wires. Cut an-

Fig. 118. Three-toed turtle.

other wire for the tail and one for the head and neck, and sharpen. From a piece of balsa, or soft wood, shape a core that will fit snugly into the shell. Run a wire up through each of the legs starting at the bottom of the foot from the outside. Turn back the skin, rub wax on the wires to make them adhesive, and wind fine tow around each of the wires to replace the muscles that you cut away; do the same for the tail. Then cover the legs and tail with composition (Formula #106) and turn the legs and tail back into the skin. Figure 117 (C and D) shows the manner in which the legs, tail, and head are anchored to the wood core. [The skin and shell are not shown to simplify the illustration.] Any cavities that now show where the legs, tail, and head join the body core are modeled out (filled in) with composition.

Place the bottom plate back into position, holding it there with small wires through the holes bored in the plate and shell. Now sew the edges of the skin together, model the throat and eye cavities out with modeling wax, and set colored glass eyes of proper size and color in place from outside the skull and hold them there with wax (used also to model in and around the eyes). Shape the turtle into a characteristic pose and allow to dry; then give it a light coat of white shellac and restore the proper life colors. Figure 118 shows the three-toed turtle.

8 | TANNING

Today, very few taxidermists, either commercial or museum, do their own tanning. This is due in large part to lack of experience and cost of equipment. Tanning is a profession in itself. One could spend years in getting the proper "feel" in tanning skins for mounting. Successful results in tanning require considerable working experience in the handling of skins to get this feel—to know what to do and when to do it. Also the cost of proper equipment—vats, shakers, kickers—and chemicals involved make it too expensive for the average taxidermist.

As with taxidermy there are no "secret" methods used in tanning. Tanning involves a combination of applying chemicals that tan the skin and the beaming and working of the skin that breaks up the fibers and softens it so it can be used. This last part of the work requires hard manual labor to change a raw skin into one that is soft and pliable over its entire surface. A skin must have "life" to it before it can be mounted.

In the early days of taxidermy, skins or capes of animals were not tanned (as we know the term today)—but "pickled." In some shops skins are still pickled, especially those for game-head mounts. Even though this is a procedure I would not recommend, I have examined game-heads mounted many years ago that were pickled and are still in good condition. However, I have found others to be in very poor shape, with the hair falling out and the skin cracked. Should you desire to try your hand at tanning, I suggest you do so on a small skin, such as a raccoon, groundhog, or fox.

The necessary tools are not many, and can be made or purchased from a taxidermy supply house; the necessary chemicals can also be purchased. As with all work, good tools and proper chemicals are indispensible. Two supports (to hold skins while fleshing/shaving) must be made; the smaller, known as a fleshing

**White Tail Deer: Habitat group, winter scene. This is one of the famous
"four seasons" groups mounted by Carl Akeley in the early 1900s. The
skins were tanned, not pickled. [Field Museum of Natural History photo.]**

beam, is essential when working with small skins, and a larger one
is used with large skins. The small beam is diagramed in Figure
119; it can be made from a piece of hardwood following the dimensions given. One end is blunt and rounded over the sides so the skin
will slide easily while it is being worked. This small beam is also
shown in Figure 120, and in Figure 121 it is being used in the
fleshing/shaving of a small skin.

Illustrated in Figure 122 is the upright knife, used primarily in
special work. This knife is used in a few shops, mostly commercial
tanning companies. It can be purchased, although the average
taxidermist will find very little use for such a knife.

For large skins a larger and heavier beam may be constructed
(Fig. 123). This beam is made from a plank of hardwood; again, one
end is blunt and the sides are rounded. The height of the beam
should suit the individual working with it. Figures 124 to 127
illustrate the various uses of not only the larger beam but also the
different types of fleshing/shaving knives used when working on
large skins.

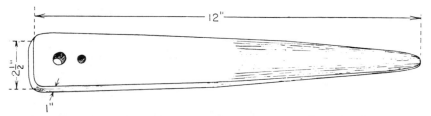

Fig. 119. Dimensions for construction of small fleshing beam.

Fig. 120. Knives used for fleshing/scraping skins.

Fig. 121. Small fleshing beam in use.

124

Fig. 122. Upright fleshing knife in use.

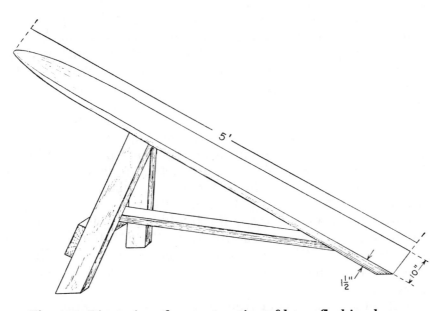

Fig. 123. Dimensions for construction of large fleshing beam.

125

PREPARING THE SKIN

Before the tanning solutions can be applied to the skin, it must be prepared. The skin should be roughly skinned out in the field as soon as the animal is collected. All surplus flesh and fat should be removed, the ears turned, the lips, eyes, and nostrils split, and all *well salted*, dried, and packed for shipment. The feet/claws should be opened down to the bone for the salt to effectively preserve the skin until it is ready for the tanning process. Field care is most important: the more care in the field, the less chance the skin will become "grease burnt" and spoiled for mounting. While in the field never dry a skin in the sun, or too near a hot fire. If you are in a wet and humid area be sure to shake out the salt each day, removing the moisture that has collected. Resalt; then again roll up the skin again, flesh side in. It may be necessary to do this several times prior to shipment. Skins that have been properly prepared in the field can be left for several years in a dry state without further damage prior to tanning and mounting. Proper field care of mammal skins have also been given in Chapter 6—Game Heads.

Dry and hard skins can be relaxed for working in a carbolic-acid-water solution (Formula #101). Leave the skin in this solution only long enough to relax. Prior to the fleshing/shaving, wash out all salt and hang the skin to allow it to drain; if the skin is large, do this several times—*all salt* must be removed at this time. The skin can now be fleshed/shaved of any remaining tissue for the tanning solutions to penetrate. Any skin, large or small, must be properly prepared for the tanning chemicals to take effect. Unless this is done, the skin will not come from the solutions tanned, as we know the term.

In the fleshing/shaving of smaller skins, it is better to work over the small fleshing beam (Fig. 121). The smaller beam can be used also when shaving around the ears, eyes, and lips of all animals; the blunt end of the beam allows you to get to the smaller and hard-to-reach areas. When working a larger skin, place it over the large beam (Figs. 124 and 125). Here the fleshing knife is being used. Figure 125 shows how the knife should be held. This angle is most important: if you are not careful, you will cut into the skin on your first attempt. It will take experience before you will skillfully handle this knife and all other types of knives used in the fleshing/shaving of skins.

Another knife used in the work is the currier's knife, illustrated in Figures 126 and 127. The skin has been placed over the large

Fig. 124. Large fleshing beam; fleshing knife in use.

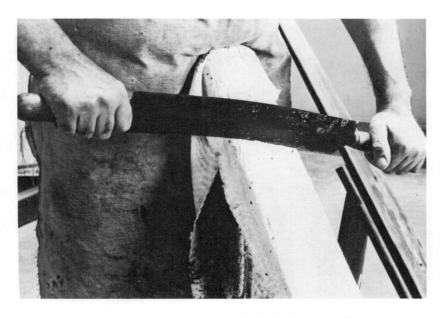

Fig. 125. Proper way to hold fleshing knife.

Fig. 126. Large fleshing beam; currier's knife in use.

Fig. 127. Proper way to hold currier's knife.

128

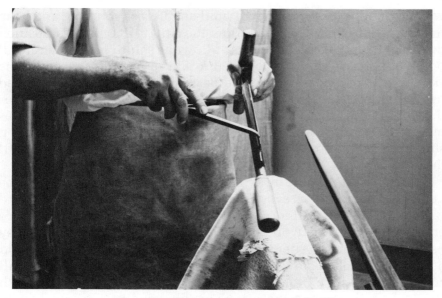

Fig. 128. Sharpening currier's knife.

beam. Figure 127 clearly shows the proper handling of the knife while working (fleshing/shaving) the skin. Figure 128 shows the knife being sharpened.

TANNING WITH THE ''PICKLE'' SOLUTION

After all surplus fat, muscle, and inner skin tissue have been removed, the skin must be degreased. Soak smaller skins in naphtha, making certain they are well covered; work each skin thoroughly in the solution. Large skins can be stretched out on a table or the floor, and the naphtha sponged on; use coarse sawdust to absorb any surplus solution. Sawdust rubbed well into the skin will absorb the naphtha and any grease. Now shake or beat out the sawdust and wash the skin in several changes of clear, cold water to remove any salt and sawdust remaining.

After the skin has been thoroughly fleshed/shaved, degreased, and washed, it can be stretched out on a table or floor, flesh side up, and wet down with the *pickle* solution (Formula #111). Sprinkle a small amount of coarse sawdust over the flesh side and again wet it down with the solution, making certain that all parts of the skin are well covered. The sawdust will hold any excess solution, and keep it from running off the skin. Allow the skin to stay in this position over night, on the table or floor, to allow the solution to penetrate all pores of the skin, but do not let the skin dry out. Now, while the skin is still damp, brush on the flesh side a coat of sulphonated neat's-foot oil solution (Formula #112). Hang the skin up until it is thoroughly dry, then dampen with the carbolic-acid solution (Formula #101), allowing this solution to relax the skin. Afterward it should be rolled up, flesh side in, and laid away over night, or until the skin is relaxed.

It is now ready to be worked over the large beam with the hands, stretching it in every way until it is soft and pliable. Hard work, yes, but this is the "secret" of tanning. All skins, to be properly tanned, must be worked, or beamed, then stretched until they have "life" to them. After working the skin over the beam, it should be soft and pliable. Now lay it hair side up and sprinkle on a small amount of naphtha. Be careful not to let the naphtha get on the flesh side or it will remove the oil. Now rub sawdust into the hair to cleanse; afterward you should beat (using a small stick) and shake out the sawdust from the hair, which "fluffs" it up. Large skins must again be dampened with the carbolic-acid-water solution (Formula #101), rolled up, and left over night or longer until pliable; then they will be ready for a final fleshing/shaving over the large beam. Use extreme care at this stage not to put cuts in the skin. Next lay out the skin on the table or floor and sponge on a mild solution of warm, soapy water; roll up, flesh side in, and lay away over night. It may be necessary, the next day, if the skin still feels stiff, to give it a coat of the sulphonated oil (Formula #112). The "pickle" tanning method is now complete. If the skin was properly prepared prior to being tanned with the chemicals, it will be soft and pliable for mounting and/or making up into a rug.

ALUM TANNING

Alum tanning is an easier method to tan or leather skins; although it is an old method, it is still being used today by some commercial tanners. First relax the skin by covering the flesh side with sawdust that has been soaked in the carbolic-acid-water solution (Formula #101). In this way the skin will absorb the moisture slowly. A large or thick skin must be immersed in a vat or tank of some sort with the carbolic-acid solution until pliable. Then work the skin over the shaving beam as previously described. The hair or fur must be free of all dirt. Now immerse the skin in the alum solution (Formula #113), leaving it in this solution for about a week—longer for large skins.

Remove it, allow it to drain, and then apply a coat of the sulphonated neat's-foot oil-water solution (Formula #112) and allow it to dry for several days. Relax the skin again with the carbolic-acid solution, either by brushing on the flesh side as with small skins or by immersing the larger ones and working them over the large beam until pliable. You may decide that the skin should again go through the process of shaving, oiling, and working to make it extra soft and pliable; do this now. When the skin is dry, dampen it again with the carbolic water solution and gradually work it over the beam until pliable. Finally, clean the hair or fur with sawdust and naphtha.

If you have used the alum solution carefully, if you have prepared the skin properly to absorb this solution, and if you have worked/beamed the skin thoroughly, you will have a well-tanned skin. The flesh side will be white all over, and it will be soft and pliable. It can now be placed over a full mammal or game-head form.

TANNING TO REMOVE THE HAIR

Tanning the skin, and at the same time removing the hair or fur, requires a different technique and formula. The skin must first be relaxed, fleshed/shaved as previously described, then immersed in a dehairing solution (Formula #114). This will remove the hair and leave the skin clean on both the hair and flesh sides. Be sure the skin is free of all dirt, salt, and fat before placing it in the solution. Soak the skin until the hair is loose. Scrape it off by placing the skin over the large beam; push—do not cut—the hair off using the currier's knife. If the hair does not come off easily, put the skin back in the solution and repeat the process. After all hair has been removed, wash the skin thoroughly in warm water to remove the lime and excess solution.

Some of the solution will remain in the skin no matter how well it is washed, so now a neutralizing solution must be used (Formula #115). The lime in the skin must be neutralized by soaking the skin over night in this solution; work it well with your hands while it is in the solution. Again wash the skin in several changes of clear, cold water. Proceed with the tanning as described, but add *15 grams chrome alum* (*dissolved*) to the tanning liquid [when the skin is tanned using the pickle solution (Formula #111)].

TANNING SMALL SKINS

A simple method for the tanning of small skins, such as rabbits, squirrels, musk-rats, so the fur will remain in place and the pelt soft and flexible.

Mix

> Soft water, 1-gallon
> Sulfuric-acid, 1 oz., commercial strength
> Salt, 1 quart

Soak skin in this solution for about three days; longer for larger skins. Remove, wring dry then soak over-night in a pail of water adding ½-cup sal soda. This neutralizes any remaining acid. Now rub and stretch skin until dry and soft; if too hard, dampen and work again and repeat until skin keeps soft and pliable when fully dry.

TANNING SNAKE SKINS

The tanning of snake skins is not only difficult but many times most disappointing; you will encounter many different types of skins and problems. Many formulas have been worked out and tried, but none so far has proved fully successful. The following procedure will work on some skins, but not on others.

If the skin is old and dry, soak it in warm water until soft; if the skin is fresh, this need not be done. Flesh the skin of all inner tissue, but use extreme care not to cut the skin; then place it in a solution of lime and water (Formula #116). Allow the skin to soak in this solution for several days, depending on the size of the skin. As soon as the scales come loose, *but no longer*, scrape them off the skin with a stiff brush. *All scales must be removed* at this time—otherwise, the tanning solution will not work. Now all lime must be removed from the skin by soaking it in the neutralizing solution (Formula #115). Next place the skin in the salt and alum solution

(Formula #117) and allow it to remain there three or four days. Remove the skin from this solution and dissolve *5 grams sodium carbonate* in a glass of warm water and add this to the solution a drop at a time, taking approximately 20 minutes to add all of it. Again immerse the skin in the solution and leave it for six more days, stirring several times each day so the solution reaches all parts. The skin now can be removed, drained, and then soaked over night in a weak solution of sulphonated oil (*1 part oil to 3 parts water*). Squeeze the liquid from the skin, stretch it, tack it out on a long board, and let it dry thoroughly. Be sure in tacking out the skin that it is stretched evenly and all wrinkles are worked out. When dry, remove the skin and work it over the beam until soft and pliable. Next, go over it with a warm—not hot—iron until smooth. To put a finished look to the skin, give it a very thin coat of liquid celluloid (one can experiment with other liquids to give the same effect) on the pattern side to give it a new and glossy look.

As previously stated, the tanning of skins requires more labor than formulas. Unless the skin is properly prepared in the salting, relaxing, and fleshing/shaving stages—before the tanning chemicals are applied and the skin is worked and beamed—it will not be properly tanned. Tanning amounts to hard, manual labor.

CHROME TANNING MAMMAL SKINS WITH HAIR

This section was written by Dominick Villa, formerly Chief Tanner, Field Museum of Natural History, who tanned many of the mammal skins mounted and installed in the habitat groups on exhibit there.

Heavy skins/hides should be tanned separately from small and medium-sized skins. Chrome tanning is always done by immersion; strong, soft, and permanent leather can be made by carefully following this method. It is *important* to prepare all skins properly (cleaning, fleshing, shaving) before tanning.

Do not tan skins for mounting with chrome. The color of chrome does not affect hair on white skins. The quantity of materials given here are for small and medium-sized skins and based on each gallon of water used as needed. If skins are very greasy, wash with soap and warm water, rinse well in clear water until all soap is out, then soak in the following solution:

Water, 1 gallon
Salt, 6 ounces
Alum, 2 to 3 ounces (according to thickness of skin)
Carbolic-acid, ¼ ounce (by volume)

Do not use a metal container, and stir skins occasionally while in the solution. Leave in this solution for one or two days. If other scraping is necessary, drain skins over the tank and finish scraping. Put skins back into the solution; and for each gallon of solution you now have, dissolve 10 grams of preparation known by its trade name, KROME TAN* in boiling water for 10 minutes using one large cup of water for each 10 grams. Add half of this mixture to the alum and salt solution without removing the skins; stir frequently. Add the other half of the mixture the following day.

Wait three or four days. Then, for each gallon of the solution, dissolve 5 grams sodium carbonate, using one large cup of hot water for each 5 grams. Add this to the solution very slowly by punching a small hole in the bottom of an empty can fixed above the solution container. Let the dissolved soda drip into the tanning solution without removing the skins, but keep stirring to prevent a foam and milklike color formation. Leave the skins in this solution five or six days longer (more time for larger skins), stirring several times each day. In cold weather chrome is slow to penetrate.

Now remove the skins and rinse in clear water. Wring them out, and while still wet brush on the following oil mixture:

2 parts warm water (by measure)
1 part sulphonated neat's-foot oil (by measure)
1 part nonsulphonated neat's-foot oil (by measure)

For each gallon of the oil mixture, add a quarter-ounce carbolic acid by volume. Hang the skins to dry completely over wood poles. Now lay out the dried skins; and using a sponge, dampen on the flesh side with carbolic-acid-water.** Fold the skin and put it in an empty barrel or other container that can serve as a "damp box" and completely cover it with an oil cloth or plastic material. It is important to keep the moistened skins from drying out.

The next day work the skin soft by stretching and pulling over the fleshing beam and working with the fleshing knife. Breaking

* KROME TAN is the trade name of a regular chrome material in powder form. It can be purchased from several taxidermy supply houses.
** Carbolic-acid-water is made by adding ½ ounce (by volume) carbolic acid to each gallon of water.

up and making the skin pliable at this time is most important in tanning—and must be done. In large tanneries this is referred to as "staking." The idea of breaking up/stretching the skin is to separate the fibers so the oil will penetrate and the skin will soften. This will work provided the skins are conditioned—not too wet, not too dry.

Now the skins must be "drumned." Run them in this machine for two or more hours with dry sawdust. It is better if several skins are put in the drum at the same time. Be sure they are only slightly damp when you first put them in; do not crowd the drum. After drumning, remove the skins and cage, or beat out, the sawdust. They are now ready for the final shaving.

Skins of foxes, rabbits, and opossums, for example, should be fleshed before tanning; others, like deer, flat skins, wolves, and bear skins, should only be scraped before tanning and shaved after tanning. Soak the flesh side with the carbolic-acid-water using a sponge; be careful not to wet the hair. Fold the skin tightly and place it back in the damp box. Keep it well covered so the water can penetrate. The next day, with the skin held over the beam, shave it with a hand-shaving knife.

After the skin is well shaved, it must be neutralized by soaking and washing it in a solution of one ounce Borax to one-half cup soap powder for each gallon of water used. Now rinse in clear water and wring it out. Nail it out on a board, stretching the skin as much as is possible. Dry the skin in this position (those that will be used for fur can be hung on poles to dry). Now finish the dried skins by running in the drum for two hours or more with dry sawdust.

Skins tanned by the above method will have a much better appearance than the regular "skin dressing." With chrome it is important to dry the skins by nailing them out on a stretching board. Even small skins will look much better—they will be finished in a nice, flat shape, and be usable as rugs.

9 | NOVELTIES

Many useful and attractive novelties can be made from the antlers or horns of deer, elk, and other types of exotic big game. It is best to secure antlers from animals that have been shot, but shed horns can be used if they have not been exposed too long to the weather. Shed horns may be checked, but these checks can be filled in with a paste made of whiting mixed with white shellac. Allow the paste to dry; then color with oil colors to the desired shade. If using antlers from a freshly killed animal, they need only be washed in warm, soapy water, dried, and then gone over with an old toothbrush dipped in raw linseed oil, working the oil well into all parts of the antlers. After the surplus oil has been wiped off using a soft, clean cloth, the antler will have a luster and lifelike coloring. Another application is a mixture of 1 part Japan to 4 parts turpentine, rubbed on with a cloth, then wiped off and polished.

What-Not (Figure 129)

This wall rack requires antlers that are symmetrical, with opposite tines, or prongs, on line with one another. Bore a 1-inch hole in the base of each antler to a depth of 3 inches. Now set a $\frac{1}{2}$-inch stove bolt in this hole, with the threaded end protruding, and anchor the bolt securely with papier-mâché or plastic wood. The shelves can be of plywood or other $\frac{3}{8}$-inch stock, and the wall panel of $\frac{3}{4}$-inch stock with the face beveled on the four edges for attractiveness. Bolt the antlers to the panel, then bolt the shelves to the tines. Stain, shellac, and varnish panel prior to fastening antlers.

Table Lamp (Figure 130)

This unique lamp has an antler for a base; the antler with the tines so branched out will support the lamp, as illustrated. Generally it is necessary to bolt on another section of antler to get this necessary support. A hole is drilled in the base of the antler, of the size of the lamp socket, and this socket is fastened with papier-mâché or plastic wood. The lamp cord extends down outside the antlers.

Hat Rack (Figure 131)

The panel for this hat rack can be purchased from taxidermy supply houses, or can be cut out to size and shape illustrated, with the face edges beveled or molded on a shaper. Select an appropriate pair of antlers that are joined by a section of the skull. After cleaning, the bone is cut along the lines as shown and fastened to the panel by two brass or nickeled wood screws. If desired, three separate tines can be cut from another antler. Bore a hole in the base of each, set in a small bolt, and anchor with plastic wood; then bolt each to the panel as illustrated.

Desk Lamp and Writing Set (Figure 132)

The base for this novel lamp requires a pair of antlers with tines of corresponding form. Bore a hole in the base of each and set a $\frac{1}{2}$-inch stove bolt into each hole. Now fasten the two antlers securely to a $\frac{3}{4}$-inch-thick baseboard. The space between the antlers is built up with papier-mâché of very thick consistency; while the mâché is still soft, place an ink bottle in the center. Allow the mâché to set and dry thoroughly; then shellac and color with oil colors. The shade, which may be a tin can cut in half lengthwise and painted, is held to the tips of the antlers, the two longer tines, with appropriate-length stove bolts.

Foot Stool (Figure 133)

The top of the stool is a piece of $\frac{3}{4}$-inch wood stock. Legs are formed by two pair of antlers of approximate size. They can be attached to the wood base by anchoring with stove bolts. Also, the antlers can

WHAT-NOT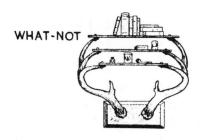

Fig. 129. What-not made from well-formed antlers.

TABLE LAMP

Fig. 130. One antler with another section bolted on.

HAT RACK

Fig. 131. From large antlers, with symmetrical tines.

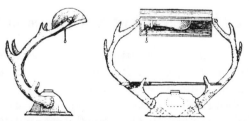

DESK LAMP AND WRITING SET

Fig. 132. Made from pair of slim antlers.

FOOT STOOL

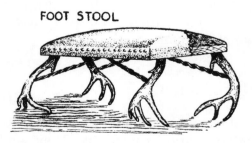

Fig. 133. Antlers must be heavy for support.

be left attached to a section of the skull, and the skull anchored to the base. The legs are braced by twisted iron bands run diagonally as illustrated. The top of the stool is padded with excelsior, then covered with upholstering leather, and fastened with brass-headed tacks driven into the edge of the board.

Ash Tray (Figure 134)

The ash tray is made from a pair of antlers from a spike buck. Bore a $\frac{1}{2}$-inch hole in the base of each antler and set in a $\frac{1}{4}$-inch stove bolt with papier-mâché or plastic wood. Make, or purchase, a brass ash tray with a detachable top, and fasten it to the side of the antlers after adjusting them to be even on a flat surface.

Deer Foot Lamp (Figures 135 to 141)

The feet of deer and similar animals, as with their antlers, can be used for many different novelties. Remove the four feet as soon as you skin out the deer; make certain to leave each foot long enough for the novelty planned. Separate the skin from the leg bone by making a cut up the back of the leg [Fig. 135 (A–B)]. Leave the joint attached (shown at dotted line), but cut the bone at an angle [Fig. 135 (C)]. Work the skin well down to the hoof but leave enough bone attached and leave skin attached to the hoof, as illustrated. Cut away the dew claws from the leg bones, leaving them attached to the skin. Now salt the skins thoroughly and have them tanned. After tanning, the leg skins and attached bones can be stored in a saturate solution of borax to which a few drops of carbolic acid have been added; keep the skins in this solution until ready for use. Now from a taxidermy supply house order the following:

    1 wood core for a 4-leg lamp
    1 inside cap plate
    1 lamp cap plate (2$\frac{1}{2}$-inch)
    1 harp holder for single-socket lamp
    1 pull-chain socket
    2 gimp bands

The wood core comes sawed in sections ready for use (Fig. 136). Pull each section apart and use for each leg. In Figure 137 the wood

ASH TRAY

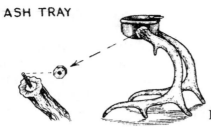

Fig. 134. From spike buck antlers.

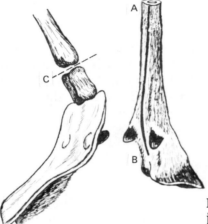

Fig. 135. Incision on leg (*A—B*); disjointed leg bone (*C*).

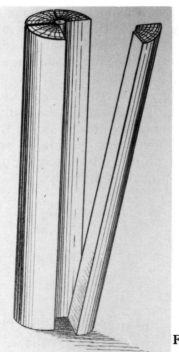

Fig. 136. Wood core for deer foot lamp.

140

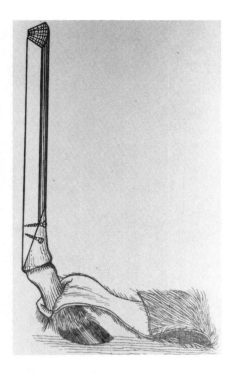

Fig. 137. Skin and foot fastened to wood core.

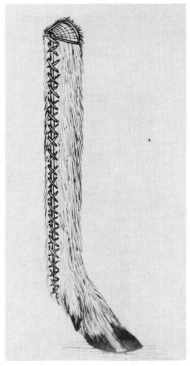

Fig. 138. Leg skin sewn together over core.

141

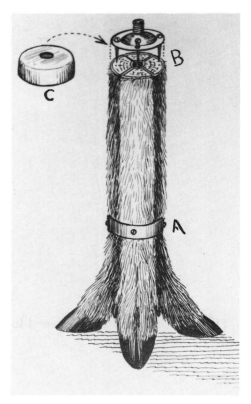

Fig. 139. Deer foot assembled for lamp.

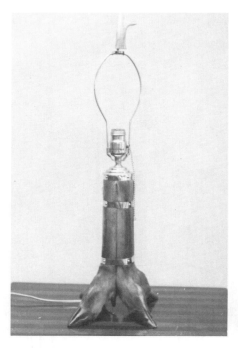

Fig. 140. Deer-foot lamp (without shade).

Fig. 141. Deer-foot lamp, complete.

Fig. 142. Thermometer, made from deer foot; leg was not skinned— poisoned, then allowed to dry.

core and leg bone have been miter-sawed and assembled with wood screws. Do this with each of the four feet, making sure that bone and core fit close together. If there are any gaps between bone and core, fill in with papier-mâché or plastic wood. While the filler is still soft, draw the skin up over the leg bone and core, and sew as indicated (Fig. 138). A little modeling of the plastic or mâché, while still soft, will give a snugger fit.

Use care when triming off excess skin at the top, making certain each leg is of the same height. If not, saw the wood core to even it off. All legs must be of the same height. Next, fasten all four legs together using one of the gimp bands [Fig. 139 (A)]. The lamp standard is now complete. Next, to wire the assembly, first attach the inside cap plate [Fig. 139 (B)] with screws as indicated, then place the outside cap plate over it [Fig. 139 (C)]. The lamp cord is brought up through the center space between the four legs (do this prior to putting on the inside cap plate) and wired to the socket assembly, which in turn screws onto the threaded part of the cap plate. The shade support may rest directly upon the light bulb, or of the type as shown in Figure 140. As a finishing touch, drill a small section of antler to fit over the bolt that projects upward from the support (Fig. 140). You can purchase the lamp shade from a taxidermy supply house (many carry a complete line) or you can make your own from a piece of leather laced with a leather throng. The completed lamp is shown in Figure 141.

Deer Foot Thermometer (Figure 142)

The thermometer is made from the foot of a large, buck deer without skinning the leg. The foot is dried slowly, then soaked in a borax-carbolic-acid-formaldehyde solution (Formula #104). It is left in this solution for several hours, then dried, and the crystals that form are brushed off. The thermometer part is secured with two brass brads. The hoof is polished prior to fastening the thermometer. The top, or cap, is cut and shaped from a piece of skin. Completed thermometer is shown in Figure 142.

INDEX